Brazil

D0096473

The 1950s were coming to a close when the world first heard the term bossa nova on João Gilberto's album *Chega de Saudade*; between 1958 and 1970 a generation of superstars wowed the world with their acrobatic and explosive football, while Oscar Niemeyer and Lúcio Costa created Brasilia, the 20th century's largest concrete utopia, situated dramatically between the blue of the sky and the green of the forest. Music, football and architecture, Brazil's three great contributions to those years of dreams and dynamism, from a country that had found its own path into the future with a 'modernity that was fluid, light and simultaneously complex'. Not even the dictatorship was able to stifle the air of optimism and revolution that combined with Brazil's legendary joy tinged with melancholy to create a soft power that was so seductive that for many years it survived its own decline. For outsiders, who were also misled by the economic boom and reforms of the 2000s – which saw the Brazilian middle classes grow at a rate unequalled almost anywhere at any time – it was a rude awakening to witness the election of a president who was greeted by half the country with a mixture of resignation and disbelief, their mood so succinctly captured by the famous hashtag #EleNão (#NotHim). The dream has turned into a nightmare; the world looks on helplessly as deforestation ravages the Amazon, which even as recently as the end of the 20th century had seemed almost infinite. But in Brazil people's lives have adapted to a different reality (or failed to) for some time: crippling corruption, the myth of a post-racial society that is debunked by blatant discrimination along with decades of a growth in violence that gives the country the unenviable record of having the world's highest number of murders. Luckily Brazilians have not lost their desire to fight, minorities are still determined to assert their rights and, now that the glorious past is dead and buried, a desire to rebuild for the future is emerging. The challenge of telling the story of this extraordinary country right now lies in searching for the thread of joy running through the sadness: *chega de saudade*, no more blues.

Contents

The photographs in this issue were taken by the Brazilian photojournalist **André Liohn**, whose work has appeared in *Der Spiegel*, *L'Espresso*, *Time*, *Le Monde* and *Veja*. After turning his hand to photography in his thirties, he quickly found a mentor in the American-Czech photographer Antonín Kratochvíl, who took him under his wing. In 2011 Liohn became the first Latin American photographer to receive the Robert Capa Gold Medal and to be nominated for the Bayeux Calvados-Normandy Award for his documentary efforts during the second Libyan civil war. His photographs of the war zone were used by the International Committee of the Red Cross for its Health Care in Danger initiative, which highlighted the violence suffered by healthcare personnel around the world. In 2012 he took part in Almost Dawn in Libya, a project that used photojournalism as a bridge for reconciliation in post-war Libya.

Brazil in Numbers

VANITY

Millions of cosmetic surgery procedures (2017)

1. USA	//////////////////////// —	4.21
2. Brazil	▬▬▬▬▬ ———	**2.52**
3. Japan	/////// ———————	1.13
4. Italy	////// ———————	0.95
5. Mexico	////// ———————	0.92
6. Russia	////// ———————	0.89
7. India	////// ———————	0.87

SOURCE: ISAPS

BOVINE POPULATION

Head of cattle in millions and as % of global total (2018)

Total world inventory: 1,001,841,000

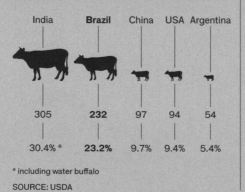

India	Brazil	China	USA	Argentina
305	**232**	97	94	54
30.4% *	**23.2%**	9.7%	9.4%	5.4%

* including water buffalo

SOURCE: USDA

SLAVERY

Estimate of the numbers of Africans transported as slaves in millions (1525–1866)

Taken from Africa: 12.5

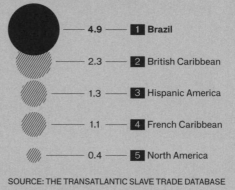

4.9	1	Brazil
2.3	2	British Caribbean
1.3	3	Hispanic America
1.1	4	French Caribbean
0.4	5	North America

SOURCE: THE TRANSATLANTIC SLAVE TRADE DATABASE

UP, UP AND AWAY

With a fleet of around 500 helicopters and 2,200 flights a day, São Paulo has more heliports than any other city in the world.

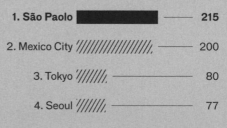

1. São Paolo	▬▬▬▬▬ —	**215**
2. Mexico City	/////////////// —	200
3. Tokyo	//////// —	80
4. Seoul	//////// —	77

SOURCE: CNBC.COM

TRAFFIC CONGESTION

Longest traffic jams of all time

`Length in km`

1. São Paolo - June 2014

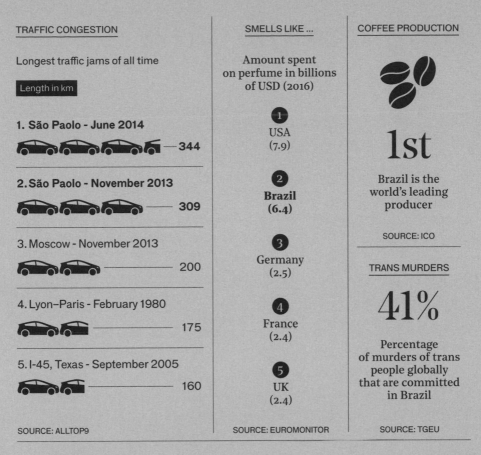 — 344

2. São Paolo - November 2013

309

3. Moscow - November 2013

200

4. Lyon–Paris - February 1980

175

5. I-45, Texas - September 2005

160

SOURCE: ALLTOP9

SMELLS LIKE ...

Amount spent
on perfume in billions
of USD (2016)

1 USA (7.9)

2 **Brazil** (6.4)

3 Germany (2.5)

4 France (2.4)

5 UK (2.4)

SOURCE: EUROMONITOR

COFFEE PRODUCTION

1st

Brazil is the
world's leading
producer

SOURCE: ICO

TRANS MURDERS

41%

Percentage
of murders of trans
people globally
that are committed
in Brazil

SOURCE: TGEU

EXPORTS OF FOOTBALLERS

Origins of footballers playing abroad (2018)

	Number playing abroad	Principal destination
Brazil	1,236	Portugal
France	821	England
Argentina	760	Chile
Serbia	465	Bosnia and Herzegovina
England	431	Scotland

SOURCE: CIES FOOTBALL OBSERVATORY

A Sign of the Times

FABIAN FEDERL
Translated by Stephen Smithson

Standing in line outside the Bar da Dona Onça, a young woman leans towards her boyfriend and whispers, 'Hey, isn't that the *telenovela* actress in front of us?' The boyfriend nods. Meanwhile a waitress has pressed a little sign into the actress's hand with a number denoting her place in the queue.

It's all quite egalitarian in what is probably central São Paulo's best-known restaurant. All must wait their turn, even soap stars, footballers and musicians from the well-to-do parts of the city. A model leans against a column while his collar is adjusted by an ostentatiously hip photographer. In the queue two men in the uniform of black ankle-skimming trousers, granny glasses and hessian *New Yorker* tote bags are discussing whether it was the *Guardian* or *The New York Times* that described the Edifício Copan, the large, grey, curvaceous high-rise on whose ground floor the Bar da Dona Onça is located, as 'Latin America's coolest building'.

Just fifteen years ago the area around the Copan was the most dangerous place in São Paulo, and the Copan itself was a particularly hazardous place to be. Today the building has become something of a new hub, the focal point of all that makes visiting the city worth while – theatres, concert halls, restaurants, bars, parties, galleries and parks – and, more generally, of all that gives it its sheer scale, something that surrounds you every second that you spend here.

The design of the building, with its curving lines hinting at the mathematical symbol for a sine, is actually modelled on the tilde above the 'a' in São [Paulo]. It was designed in the 1950s by Oscar Niemeyer, Latin America's most renowned architect, and is the largest residential property in the world in terms of living space. Some of its apartments cover several hundred square metres while others are so small that they require folding beds. For tourists looking to stay at the Copan, a range of accommodation types can be found listed on Airbnb.

The Copan is like a small town within a big city. In the arcades on the ground floor there are seventy-two shops, travel agencies, an evangelical free church, two galleries – as well as popular establishments such as the Bar da Dona Onça, where everything, from the napkins to the frames of the photomontages on the walls, is decorated with kitschy leopard print. During the day throngs of people – residents, passers-by and tourists – move between the arcades, past enamel signs from the 1960s telling you where you are, past dozens of porters who know their residents by sight and will hold the lift doors open for them, past groups of office workers from the nearby office blocks.

It is often said that São Paulo has no views of the horizon because there's always a building in the way, but you can ignore such talk if you stand on the right floor of the Copan. With a little luck – and with no rain, smog or haze – you can see from here to the line of hills on the northern fringes of the twenty-million megalopolis. Given the scale, it is easy to feel like a farmer's boy in the big city, mesmerised by the endless chains of brilliant car headlights, the clusters of high-rise buildings, the

hundreds of helicopters and aeroplanes in the airspace above the city. Depending on your vantage point you might see the eight-lane Rua da Consolação, which leads to the rich southern part of the city, or you might see the Minhocão. This long thoroughfare – the 'Earthworm' – is closed to traffic at weekends when it is transformed into São Paulo's most popular leisure area, bringing the city's residents out to walk their dogs, to skateboard or to cycle. The walls of the buildings, which in some cases are just a few centimetres from the roadside, are covered in street art, while notices stuck to lamp posts carry political propaganda or advertisements for readings of tarot cards and coffee grounds. On Sundays tens of thousands of people walk down the Minhocão to the weekly market at Santa Cecilia to drink sugar-cane juice and eat pastel de feira, fried empanadas, the greasiest – and thus also arguably the best – that the city has to offer. The Earthworm leads from Praça Roosevelt, a square right next to the Copan around which teenagers and students sit with cans of beer in the evening, to Campos Elíseos, another central district, about two kilometres away.

The streets are narrower in Campos Elíseos than in the rest of São Paulo, but they are less densely built up. There you can still find the 19th-century villas built by the coffee barons when the city became rich on the cultivation and export of coffee, all done out in colonial style and surrounded by magnificent gardens. At the same time Campos Elíseos is one of the most run-down parts of the city. It may house the Estação da Luz – an ornate former railway station now converted into a concert hall with among the best acoustics in the world, to which guest conductors from New York or Tokyo are routinely flown in – but you only have to walk five metres from the entrance and you'll find tents and tarpaulins stretched out, underneath which there are rows of people – hundreds, maybe a thousand – wrapped in grey blankets. Some of them pull nervously on glass pipes; others swap small rocks of crack for a few coins. Several kick cans around; some call out in confusion; others lie, bent double, in the middle of the street. Up to three thousand *craqueiros* – crack addicts – are based around here.

Campos Elíseos provides a visible reminder of what it was like fifteen years ago in and around the Edifício Copan. One person who can tell you about those dark times is Affonso de Oliveira, now chief caretaker at the Copan. He sits at his desk on the first floor of the building, a broad, tall man of seventy-nine with white hair and a rumbling voice. Before him there are piles of books – about architecture, about urban planning and also about the Copan. On the wall behind him hang panoramic photos from the roof terrace, old clocks and calendars and a floor plan showing the positions of the original lifts from the 1950s – all gifts from residents. On Affonso's belt the walkie-talkie crackles at regular intervals; this time it is assistant caretaker Luis, one of 103 employees, looking for plans for the defective power lines in Block B. On the table the phone is vibrating. Every few minutes the secretary brings him sheets of paper covered in notes.

Affonso has witnessed the fall and rise of the building right from the beginning. In 1963, when he moved in, he was a chemistry student and the Copan was still a prestigious building. São Paulo, the administrative centre of large-scale agriculture in the region, was in the ascendant and would, it was believed, become to Brazil what New York was to the United States. Actors, musicians and artists lived in the Copan; the great Tropicália musician Caetano Veloso sang songs about the neighbourhood. But then came the urban exodus of the 1980s, when those who had money moved to the country, leaving poverty to become concentrated in the centre.

'In 1993 crack arrived,' says Affonso. 'At that time there was a woman on my floor with two children of primary-school age. Every evening I would see the boys sitting by themselves in the empty corridor in front of the apartment door while the mother received clients inside.' On the floor below was a military policeman who sold crack. Again and again people died: some overdosed; some were killed; many fell to their deaths from the roof, whether in a drugged frenzy or because they'd had enough of life. Again and again fires broke out. In the mid-1990s all the shops in the ground-floor arcades were closed.

Affonso did not want to see his home deteriorate any further, so he applied for the position of caretaker and set about the task of renewal. He called the porters of the five blocks A–E to his office and set up a log of those residents who received new 'friends', 'contacts' or 'colleagues' every few hours. He issued daily warnings to drug dealers and prostitutes that he would call the police. Many thought he was bluffing, but Affonso was serious. He was threatened and harassed; he would move through the Copan armed and in a bulletproof vest. He started putting up cameras in the arcades and in front of the doorways, then on the surrounding streets. 'The dealers eventually left the Copan because it had started to become too troublesome for them here,' he says. 'Without dealers there were no *craqueiros*, without *craqueiros* there was no crime and without crime there was no fear.'

People working in the headquarters of big companies in the city centre began to feel safe again around the Copan. By around 2007 the area was starting to fill up

at lunchtimes. More and more restaurants opened. As well as the Bar da Dona Onça these included the Padaria Santa Efigênia, also situated right inside the Copan. This is a 'bakery' of a kind typically found in São Paulo, which means that it's more a kind of restaurant/bakery/café/kiosk/bar/ souvenir shop.

Two hundred metres away, on Praça Roosevelt, the first clubs soon began to open up, bringing people from richer neighbourhoods to the centre for nights out. Some of these 'nightlife commuters' eventually started to look for somewhere to live near the *praça*, and the best place for that was the Copan. Students and artists followed, and after them a more bourgeois clientele. By 2018 the Copan was roughly back where it started. This is the year when its arcades – a meeting place in the 1960s for artists who would later go on to exhibit in New York and London – saw the opening of their first bar with international flair.

At the entrance to the Fel you have to give your name, and then you will be led in by a waiter in a suit. The Fel is set out in a sombre manner, brownish-red hues with small spherical lamps giving off just a little light – dim and subdued as though it were emitted reluctantly – into the room. Here you won't find caipirinhas or vodka-cola. You will find drinks with history, such as the St Charles punch – port, sherry, raspberry and lemon, created in the bar of the Hotel St Charles in New Orleans in 1896 – or the Saratoga – Woodford Reserve bourbon, Carpano vermouth and Angostura bitters – first concocted in 1862 in his Broadway bar by Jerry Thomas, the pioneer of the American art of mixing cocktails.

The Fel, unlike other establishments housed within the Copan, is not at all kitschy or daring, it is stylish. You sit on sumptuously upholstered barstools with the massive building above you, and you could be in New York or London rather than São Paulo. But then you lean back against one of the columns studded with small terrazzo tiles, seventy-two million of which were ordered in an act of *folie de grandeur* for the Copan façade, and you couldn't be anywhere else.

The Icon: Marta Vieira da Silva

The number 10 printed on the back of a football shirt didn't have much significance before the arrival of Pelé. The greatest player of all time was given the number (purely by chance, apparently) during the 1958 World Cup when he exploded on to the world scene as a precocious seventeen-year-old and created the mystical aura that now surrounds the number. A constellation of other football stars followed, including Zico and Zidane, Platini and Messi, Maradona and Neymar, to name but a few.

But none of these other number 10s has had so long and hard a road to follow as Marta Vieira da Silva.

Born into poverty in the *sertão* – or outback – in the Northeast region of the country, she put all her tenacity, bravery and talent into pursuing her dream of becoming a professional footballer. She achieved this without the support she was due but to great acclaim: in her nineteen-year career she has been voted the best footballer in the world six times by FIFA, a number equalled only by Lionel Messi – and she got there first.

It would be fair to say that Marta practically invented the women's game in Brazil. Navigating her way through one of the most male-dominated societies on the planet, which has done everything in its power to prevent women from playing its sacred sport, she rose to become a footballing idol wearing the most famous number-10 shirt of all, that of the Brazilian *Seleção*, the national football team. Overcoming the disdain of managers and institutions, she became a heroine in the fight for gender equality.

Like millions of Brazilians she grew up in a family with an absentee father – her mother, Teresa, raised her four children alone in a single-room house partitioned with sheets hung from the ceiling. Marta, the youngest, used to watch the boys playing football from an early age and started playing herself at six, much to her mother's disapproval. 'There was a lot of prejudice. They used to call me a tomboy,' said the star player in an interview with Brazilian magazine *Trip*. 'Girls played handball and volleyball. I was the only one who played football. A lot of people used to gossip, saying things like, "How can her mother let her do that? Why don't her brothers say something?"'

Even her family was reluctant to accept her desire to play; her brothers were irritated by the constant comments, and the youngest daughter's talent would often be the cause of fights breaking out in the street. She spent much of her childhood running – either after the ball or away from the local football pitches to avoid being caught by her mother when she was

AYDANO ANDRÉ MOTTA
Translated by Laura Garmeson

spotted playing a game. 'There was a time when I would wake up at 5.30 to train with the boys. The pitch wasn't covered, so it would be too hot to play after 9 a.m. We'd get there really early, then we could play for a couple of hours at least.'

It was no easy journey from there to the professional stadiums. With no role models to follow Marta had to blaze her own trail. After training with the youth club at the Centro Sportivo Alagoano (CSA) in Maceió, the state capital and largest city in Alagoas, she did what many generations of Northeasterners had done before her and migrated to Rio de Janeiro where, aged fourteen, she began her professional career at Vasco da Gama. A left-footed player with extraordinary talent, she was on the receiving end of sexism even when her skills were recognised: 'She plays like a man,' was the highest possible praise.

Things began to change in 2004 when Marta transferred to Umeå IK in Sweden. She went on to play for Los Angeles Sol (USA), Santos (back in Brazil, where she wore the number-10 shirt immortalised by Pelé), Gold Pride (USA), New York Flash (USA), Tyrëso FF and FC Rosengård (both Swedish) before transferring to Orlando Pride in Florida. She won silver medals with the Brazilian team at the Olympic Games in Athens (2004) and Beijing (2008) and was runner-up in the final of the Women's World Cup in China in 2007.

At the 2019 World Cup in France, Marta surpassed the men yet again. When she scored in the penalty shoot-out against Italy she became the highest goal scorer in the history of the competition across both genders, beating German player Miroslav Klose's record with a total of seventeen goals. Thanks to Brazil's stubborn disdain for women's football, they fielded an inferior team compared with the likes of Germany, Sweden, Holland and the USA (who took home the title and brought striker Megan Rapinoe international fame).

After the Brazilian team was beaten by France in the knockout stages, their legendary number 10 made a speech that would go down in history. 'There's not going to be a Marta for ever, there's not going to be a Formiga for ever, there's not always going to be a Cristiane. The women's game depends on you! Value them more,' she said with tears in her eyes, referring to the other veteran players in the squad.

Marta's achievements have exceeded her wildest dreams. She became a UN ambassador for humanitarian causes, joining a group that includes actress Angelina Jolie, Queen Rania of Jordan, tennis player Maria Sharapova and model Gisele Bündchen. With an annual salary of $370,600 (her male counterpart, Messi, earns $108.6 *million*), she can make sure her mother lives comfortably, far from the poverty of her home town of Dois Riachos.

But this number 10's greatest achievement has been to pave the way for empowerment in women's football, a journey that's only just begun.

Order and Progress?

JON LEE ANDERSON

A T-shirt promoting the theme of the 2020 São Paulo carnival, chosen by the Mancha Verde samba school, winner of the 2019 event. It says: 'Father forgive them, for they know not what they do.'

Following the election of Jair Bolsonaro as president of Brazil in 2018, Jon Lee Anderson, one of the USA's foremost reporters and a leading expert on Latin America, attempts to answer the question the whole world has asked: how was this possible? An illuminating portrait of a country we thought was different.

The authoritarian leaders taking power around the world share a vocabulary of intolerance, insult and menace. Jair Bolsonaro, who was elected president of Brazil on promises to end crime, right the economy and 'make Brazil great', has spent his career gleefully offending women, black people, environmentalists and gays. 'I would be incapable of loving a homosexual son,' he has said. 'I would prefer that my son die in an accident than show up with some guy with a moustache.' As a national legislator he declared one political rival, Maria do Rosário, 'not worth raping'. Immigrants are 'scum'. The United Nations is 'a bunch of communists'. He supports the torture of drug dealers, the use of firing squads and the empowerment of a hyper-aggressive police force. 'A policeman who doesn't kill,' he has said, 'isn't a policeman.'

On New Year's Day 2019 Bolsonaro was inaugurated in the capital city of Brasilia. Standing in the back of a Rolls-Royce Silver Wraith convertible, he waved at crowds of supporters, and they shouted back, 'The captain has arrived!' 'The legend!' Bodyguards trotted alongside the car, flanked by uniformed cavalrymen on elegant white horses. Bolsonaro was sixty-three at the time, tall and slim, with sharply parted dark hair and heroically bushy eyebrows. His third wife, Michelle, stood next to him, waving at the masses. After the inaugural ceremony Bolsonaro gave a speech outside the Planalto, the presidential palace; huge video screens magnified his image for tens of thousands of supporters. Many wore Brazilian flags draped over their shoulders and T-shirts featuring the outline of Bolsonaro's face in the style of the movie poster for *The Godfather*. At the ceremony Bolsonaro had spoken broadly of the need to 'unite the people'. Now, addressing his most fervent supporters, he could relax. He said that he had come to free them from the scourge of socialism – an allusion to his left-leaning predecessors Luiz Inácio Lula da Silva and Dilma Rousseff, who had governed from 2003 to 2016. 'Our flag will never be red,' he said. 'It will be red only if we need to bleed over it.' The crowd took up a chant, 'Never red!'

A former army captain, Bolsonaro served seven undistinguished terms in the Chamber of Deputies, Brazil's highest legislative body, representing four different political parties. Over twenty-seven years he delivered some fifteen hundred speeches and introduced more than 150 bills, but only two passed – one exempting computer equipment from taxation and another approving a controversial cancer drug. Mostly, he spoke on behalf of the armed forces, even calling for a restoration of the repressive military dictatorship that governed Brazil from 1964 to 1985. In one interview, he discounted the idea that democracy could bring order and prosperity: 'You'll only change things by having a civil war and doing the work the military regime didn't do ... If a few innocent people die, that's all right.'

Like many autocrats, Bolsonaro came to power with a suddenness that alarmed the elites. He had run a low-budget campaign, consisting mostly of a social-media effort overseen by his son Carlos. At events with supporters, he posed for selfies

JON LEE ANDERSON is a journalist and war reporter who has worked for *The New Yorker* since 1998. He has written profiles of numerous public figures, including Augusto Pinochet, Fidel Castro and Gabriel García Márquez, as well as the biography *Che Guevara: A Revolutionary Life* (Grove Press USA/Bantam UK, 1997). He won the Maria Moors Cabot Prize for his reporting on Latin America.

making a gesture as if he were shooting a machine gun. He promised to 'reconstruct the country' – and to return power to a political right that had been in eclipse for decades. In the inaugural ceremony, he vowed to 'rescue the family, respect religions and our Judaeo-Christian tradition, combat gender ideology, conserving our values'.

Afterwards Bolsonaro received a procession of foreign dignitaries, and, as they stepped up to pay their respects, the crowd greeted them with cheers or boos. The Hungarian autocrat Viktor Orbán got perfunctory applause; the *bolsonaristas* seemed not to know who he was. The Israeli prime minister Benjamin Netanyahu, who at the time was fending off charges of fraud and bribery, got a riotous cheer. Bolivia's president, Evo Morales, the only left-wing leader to attend, was subjected to shouts of 'Get out, communist,' and '*índio de merda*' – 'fucking Indian'.

Despite Bolsonaro's divisive rhetoric, US conservatives were enthusiastic about his presidency. He had expressed wariness of China and hostility towards socialists in Cuba and Venezuela; he promised to move Brazil's embassy in Israel from Tel Aviv to Jerusalem. Donald Trump didn't attend the inauguration, but he tweeted his solidarity: 'The USA is with you!' Bolsonaro, who sees in Trump a kindred spirit and an opportunity, tweeted back: 'Together, under God's protection, we shall bring prosperity and progress to our people!'

*

Brasilia, built in the late 1950s, is a city of immense spaces, with sweeping lawns and public buildings in curvilinear shapes – a *Jetsons*-era vision of optimism for the future. As the seat of government it is home to tens of thousands of middle-class bureaucrats and their families. It is also a place where destitute people camp out in improvised shelters alongside highways and use grand fountains to wash their laundry. The country's population, 211.5 million people in 2019, is bitterly polarised. Violent crime is endemic. In 2017 nearly sixty-four thousand Brazilians were murdered, an average of about 175 every day. The economy, after several years of devastating recession, is virtually stagnant; 25 per cent of the population lives below the poverty line of $5.50 a day.

A decade ago Brazil was prospering, amid a boom in oil and other commodities. Luiz Inácio Lula da Silva, the president at the time, was a charismatic leftist; the son of farmworkers, he had gone from shoeshine boy to steelworker and union leader before taking office in 2003. Lula was popular, and his Workers' Party (known by its Portuguese initials PT) instituted generous domestic programmes. His administration did little to diminish Brazil's tradition of corruption, and not enough to reduce crime or develop industry, but, as long as commodities prices stayed high, the economy thrived. In 2005 his government finished paying off a $15-billion loan to the International Monetary Fund, a year ahead of schedule.

In 2010 Lula stepped aside, having reached the legal limit of two consecutive terms, and his protégée Dilma Rousseff – a leftist guerrilla in her youth – became Brazil's first female president. But commodities prices were slipping, and in her second term a corruption scandal exploded around the state-run oil company, Petrobras. Brazilians came out on to the streets to protest, and Rousseff's political rivals sensed an opportunity. In 2016 they began hearings to impeach her on charges of improperly using loans from state banks to obscure a budget deficit. Rousseff's supporters complained of hypocrisy, noting that many members of the Brazilian legislature had been indicted for crimes ranging from bribery and money laundering to kidnapping and slavery. (The legislator who led the impeachment effort, Eduardo Cunha, was subsequently convicted of taking $40 million in bribes.) But the bid to remove Rousseff worked. It also helped draw attention to Bolsonaro. During the proceedings, he dedicated his vote to Carlos Brillhante Ustra, who had commanded the military unit that captured and tortured Rousseff when she was a young guerrilla.

For Brazilians watching the news in recent years, the country can appear to be perilously in decline. An enormous scandal – called Operação Lava Jato, or Operation Car Wash – seems to involve every third official in the government (see box opposite). Two dams have collapsed at mine sites in the countryside, releasing millions of gallons of waste. In September 2018 an accidental fire broke out at the 200-year-old National Museum, destroying an irreplaceable ethnographic collection. 'The country is overwhelmed by a terrible feeling that we have failed as a nation,' Gunter Axt, a Brazilian historian, told me, 'and perhaps it is true.'

When Bolsonaro won his party's nomination in July 2018, he seemed to offer a total inversion of political power and ideology. The military, despite a constitutional mandate to stay out of politics, backed him openly, as did a raft of wealthy business interests. His strongest competitor, Lula, was sidelined; Sérgio Moro, the judge who oversaw the Car Wash trials, had sentenced him to twelve years in prison on charges of corruption and money laundering. Still, Lula retained a large lead in the polls, and he appealed to the Supreme Court to allow him to remain free so that he could run in the election. The appeal was denied a few days after the commander of the Brazilian Army suggested on Twitter that the armed forces wanted him in jail. In February 2019 Lula, who was seventy-three at the time, was given an additional thirteen-year sentence, although he was released on appeal after nineteen months. (Moro became Bolsonaro's minister of justice but quit in April 2020 after Bolsonaro fired Brazil's federal police chief, precipitating a political crisis.)

*

Bolsonaro's vice-president, Hamilton Mourão, told me that his boss's greatest virtue was his humble roots. 'People have to understand, he comes from one of the poorest parts of São Paulo state,' he said. 'He is a self-made man. He understands the problems of poor people, and he says what they want to hear.' Bolsonaro is often compared with Trump, but Mourão disputed the analogy. 'Trump has always had a lot of money,' he said. 'Bolsonaro was never rich. But both came in the moments that their countries needed them.'

Bolsonaro grew up in Eldorado, a sleepy town in Brazil's 'banana heartland' south of São Paulo. His parents, who were of Italian and German descent, moved there when he was a boy, and his father, an itinerant dentist, set up a practice. One of six children – several of whom have never left Eldorado – Bolsonaro did not get along with his father, whom he has described as a heavy drinker who inspired discord in the family. He has claimed, perhaps straining credulity, that he did not speak to his father until he was twenty-eight, at which point he stopped hoping for him to change and decided to buy him a drink; after that they became 'good friends'.

In 1970, during the first decade of military rule, a Brazilian Army unit descended on Eldorado in pursuit of Carlos Lamarca, an officer who had gone rogue and joined a Marxist guerrilla group. As the soldiers ransacked houses and searched the woods for hideouts, Bolsonaro, who was fifteen, was enthralled; he offered to help them in their search.

Three years later Bolsonaro was accepted into the army's cadet corps, and he soon transferred to the elite Agulhas Negras (Black Needles) military academy. While he was training, Brazil's army was engaged in a vicious campaign to eliminate leftists. Thousands of Brazilians were detained in secret torture centres, and more than four hundred were killed, their bodies disappeared. Bolsonaro apparently played no part in the repression, but he hasn't condemned it. He has said of the military regime that its 'biggest mistake was to torture and not kill'.

In 1985 Brazil returned to democratic rule and the military returned to its barracks. Soon afterwards Bolsonaro wrote an unauthorised magazine article in which he complained about the military hierarchy and argued for increased wages for the troops. His superiors imprisoned him for two weeks for creating an 'environment of unrest'. A year later he faced a more serious charge: as part of his campaign to increase wages, he had conspired to put pressure on commanders by setting off grenades at military garrisons around Rio. Although he proclaimed his innocence, investigators found sketches for the bombing plan drawn in his hand. Bolsonaro was

OPERATION CAR WASH

They were after a money-laundering operation that had its improbable 'headquarters' in a service station in the south of Brasilia, but the investigators – including Judge Sérgio Moro of Curitiba – discovered from the phone taps that something else was going on: the garage was also being used as a base from which to pay bribes to politicians. In the crackdown of 17 March 2014 the police discovered that the money involved led straight back to one of the bosses of the state-owned oil company Petrobras, and so, almost by chance, began the largest corruption investigation in Brazilian history, known as Lava Jato, or Car Wash – even though, ironically, there was no car wash at the garage. Over five years and hundreds of different strands of the investigation, Lava Jato revealed a colossal network of bribes passed between politicians and big business. Brazil had seen countless corruption investigations before, but, for the first time, people who had previously been untouchable were being investigated and finding themselves behind bars, including many leading Petrobras executives, the tycoon Eike Batista, the ex-governor of Rio Sérgio Cabral, the former president of the Chamber of Deputies Eduardo Cunha (who had authorised the impeachment trial of Dilma Rousseff), the former minister José Dirceu and former president Lula himself. The country's major construction companies, such as the giant Odebrecht, were also involved, revealing connections with the political classes in many other South American countries.

Above: A small amusement park set up in the city of Tatuí, São Paulo state, one of Jair Bolsonaro's electoral strongholds.
Below: A fruit seller in the centre of São Paulo. With the rise in unemployment, the number of irregular workers has increased, a cause of concern for the Bolsonaro government.

found guilty by a disciplinary committee but cleared in the Superior Military Court, where a majority of judges decided that there was insufficient evidence; he was allowed to enter the reserves as a captain, with a full pension. There were reports that Bolsonaro had been treated favourably to prevent unrest in the lower ranks – although several judges chided him for being 'consumed by vanity'.

Around that time Bolsonaro won a seat on Rio's city council, representing the Christian Democratic Party. In 1990 he was elected to the Chamber of Deputies, where he became known for intemperate behaviour, registering more disciplinary proceedings than any of his peers. In 2003 he grew violent during a dispute with the legislator Maria do Rosário, twice shoving her roughly in the chest. When she protested, he said that she was a 'slut' and told her to 'go cry'. In 2014 he called out to Rosário during a congressional session, crudely reminding her of the incident. Bolsonaro was fined $2,500 for having 'offended his colleague's honour'.

During Bolsonaro's presidential campaign, women protested his candidacy under the slogan #EleNão (#NotHim – for more on this see page 49). Nevertheless, he got more than half the female vote. When he was denounced, it often seemed only to strengthen his support. In September 2018, a month before the first round of voting, he visited the provincial city of Juiz de Fora. He was relaxed, wearing jeans and a T-shirt, as his supporters carried him through the streets on their shoulders. Suddenly, a man carrying a knife concealed in a plastic bag lurched forward and stabbed him in the stomach. The attack nearly killed Bolsonaro; his liver, lung and intestines were punctured, and he lost a great deal of blood. But it gave him a clear bounce in the polls. On 7 October he won 46 per cent of the vote. His nearest opponent – Fernando Haddad, called in at the last minute to replace the imprisoned Lula – got 29 per cent. In the second round, Bolsonaro beat Haddad again, and he began to speak of the attack in providential terms. At his inauguration, he thanked God for saving him so that he could 'carry out the honourable mission of governing Brazil'.

*

In late November 2018 Bolsonaro appeared at an anniversary celebration for Brazil's Paratrooper Infantry Brigade, from which he graduated in 1977. The brigade is stationed inside the Military Village, a fastidiously maintained complex on the run-down outskirts of Rio de Janeiro. When Bolsonaro arrived, in a procession of black SUVs, officers in camouflage swarmed around, greeting him with salutes and affectionate hugs. Bolsonaro stood at the podium, watching with satisfaction as parachutists jumped from planes and descended on to a wide lawn.

Later Bolsonaro spoke to a group of reporters, who seemed unfazed by the abuse that he habitually directed at them. One asked about rumours that he was using a colostomy bag after the assault and that he would have to undergo more surgery. He said yes, with a disdainful look. Asked whether his son Carlos might join his administration, Bolsonaro replied defensively, 'My children are still with me, without any problem. He can have a place in the government if he so desires.'

Bolsonaro's three sons from his first marriage, who are in their mid-thirties, are a central part of his political team. He calls them Zero One, Zero Two and Zero Three. Flávio, the eldest, won a seat in the Senate last year. Carlos, who helped run his father's campaign, is an alderman on the

Rio city council. Eduardo, the youngest, is possibly the most extreme of the brothers. In the impeachment proceedings against Rousseff, he stood behind his father, mouthing along with his words as he cast his vote in the name of her torturer. A former federal policeman, Eduardo recently joined the far-right organisation, the Movement, established by Steve Bannon, Trump's former chief strategist, as its Latin American representative. (Bolsonaro also has a fourth son, Renan, a law student, from his second marriage, and a young daughter, Laura, with his current wife.)

Bolsonaro's administration is heavily stocked with military leaders: eight of the twenty-two cabinet positions are filled by ex-generals. His ideas are informed by Olavo de Carvalho, a philosopher and a former astrologer who has attracted a following with eccentric interpretations of works by Machiavelli, Descartes and others. Carvalho, seventy-three, lives in Richmond, Virginia, where he identifies with American 'redneck' culture by hunting bears, smoking cigarettes and drinking. Two current cabinet ministers were appointed on his recommendation: the education minister, Ricardo Vélez Rodríguez, a conservative theologian, and the foreign minister, Ernesto Araújo. Both subscribe to Carvalho's notions that 'cultural Marxism' has contaminated Western society and that climate change is a Marxist plot. Carvalho lends a patina of intellectualism to Bolsonaro's proposals; recently Carvalho told an interviewer that Brazil's problem with violent crime might have been averted if the military regime had killed the right twenty thousand people.

*

Much of Bolsonaro's political support comes from agribusiness, the arms industry and the religious right, a nexus of power referred to as the 'Three Bs' – beef, bullets and Bibles. In Brasilia, I met with Alberto Fraga, one of his oldest friends and a close political ally, who headed the 'bullet bloc' in congress for two decades until a recent conviction on bribery charges. (Fraga successfully appealed against the decision.) In office, Bolsonaro had moved quickly to loosen gun laws, and Fraga, who was a police officer for twenty-eight years, was pleased that more people would be able to own weapons. (It was also good for business; the stock value of Taurus, Brazil's largest gun manufacturer, has doubled since Bolsonaro secured his party's nomination.) 'Guns don't increase crime,' Fraga said, 'public policies do.' He had forty-eight guns himself, he told me, shrugging. 'I like them.'

Bolsonaro posits authoritarian violence as the way to solve Brazil's crime problem. In one television interview, he said that officers who kill dozens of troublemakers 'need to be decorated, not prosecuted'. His allies, like Trump's, at least feign exasperation at their leader's rhetorical excesses. Fraga told me, 'I think that's just him talking. We need to get him to control that.' But these sorts of views are common among his loyalists. The newly elected governor of Rio de Janeiro state recently initiated a shoot-to-kill policy against armed criminals and recommended that police helicopters patrolling the *favelas* carry snipers to 'slaughter' anyone openly carrying a weapon. In February 2019 police officers in the Fallet-Fogueteiro *favela* killed thirteen young men, most of whom were reportedly executed after they had surrendered.

Bolsonaro's programmes risk giving greater licence to a police force that is famously violent and corrupt. For years, Marielle Franco, a popular left-wing city councilwoman, spoke out against

Above: The Tactical Shoot firing range in Botucatu has welcomed new members since the Bolsonaro government made it easier for civilians to buy weapons.
Below: A woman in Avenida Paulista, central São Paulo.

> 'Messages linked to Bolsonaro's campaign arrived on voters' phones, accusing PT candidates of endorsing paedophilia.'

extrajudicial killings by police officers in the city's *favelas*. In March 2018 Franco, an openly bisexual black woman, was killed in downtown Rio.

One afternoon I visited Marcelo Freixo, a 51-year-old congressman from Franco's party who has spent years investigating Rio's *milícias* – paramilitary groups, linked to the police, that compete for territory with criminal gangs in the *favelas*. Because he has received many death threats, he lives in a closely guarded building next to an army base and travels with armed guards provided by the state. He told me that he believed Franco was killed by former members of the police's Elite Squad, working for a group of hit men known as the Crime Bureau. 'Her assassination was the most sophisticated in the history of modern Rio,' he said. Franco was tracked by men driving a car with a cloned licence plate and killed with four precise shots to the head; the weapon was a submachine gun often used by Rio's military police. Freixo surmised that her killers were hired by rival politicians. 'You can't understand Rio unless you understand the organised crime here,' he said. 'Naples has nothing on us. It's not a parallel state – it *is* the state.'

Franco's killing has led to one of the Bolsonaro administration's biggest scandals, as the Brazilian press has noted links between suspects and the president's family. Flávio served in the state legislature alongside Franco, and the two sometimes clashed. Like his father, he has argued in favour of legalising the *milícias* in the hope of putting pressure on drug-trafficking gangs. In January 2019 it was revealed that Flávio had employed the wife and the mother of Adriano Magalhães da Nóbrega, a former policeman who was now the leader of the Crime Bureau. Nóbrega was wanted in connection with the killing, but he had fled before he could be detained. As an investigation began, Flávio persuaded a friendly judge to have it quashed, but another judge reversed the ruling, and the inquiry has continued. Flávio maintains that he has 'nothing to hide', and Jair Bolsonaro says that he believes his son – although he has promised to let justice take its course. Steve Bannon dismissed the case as politically motivated – a witch hunt. The forces of 'cultural Marxism', he said, had attacked the Bolsonaros, who were 'extraordinary people'.

The investigation has produced no conclusions, but there has been some political fallout. Jean Wyllys, one of the country's three openly gay lawmakers, was on a trip abroad when the news broke about Flávio's connection with the Crime Bureau. Wyllys, a friend and political ally of Franco's, announced that he would not return to Brazil; he did not want to choose between living with bodyguards and risking death. Wyllys was an antagonist of Bolsonaro's. When Bolsonaro cast his vote during Rousseff's impeachment, Wyllys spat at him. After Wyllys announced that he was not returning, Bolsonaro tweeted, 'Great Day!' with a thumbs-up emoji. Freixo, from his apartment in Rio, shot back: 'How about you start behaving like president of the republic and stop acting like a brat? Show some dignity.'

*

On the left, the new administration has inspired fears that the country is 'going back to 1964', the year that the military

THE PASSENGER   Jon Lee Anderson

seized power. But some liberals have strained to understand the new order on its own terms. One of the most visible is Fernando Gabeira, a founder of Brazil's Green Party, who is legendary for his involvement in a Marxist guerrilla group that, in 1969, kidnapped the US ambassador to Brazil. In the 1980s Gabeira gained additional celebrity by posing for seaside photographs wearing only a crocheted bikini bottom.

Gabeira is now seventy-nine. A lean man with silver hair and rimless glasses, he lives in an apartment near Ipanema beach. Working as a television interviewer, he spoke with Bolsonaro supporters during the campaign, trying to understand their motivations. Gabeira told me that he saw Bolsonaro's victory as a reaction to the 'moral collapse' of the left, owing to the PT's corruption scandals. In his view, 'the left is finished unless it deals with its failings and engages in self-criticism'. Many leftists evidently believe that the criticism is better applied elsewhere; after Gabeira had a friendly exchange with Bolsonaro on the air, he was accused of 'normalising barbarism'.

Brazil, particularly in the countryside, is a traditionalist, Catholic country, and at times the urban left has made it easy for Bolsonaro to score points. In Rio, a woman who works as a literary translator told me about a fracas in her son's public high school. Last year, amid a debate on gender identity, the chancellor decreed that the female school uniform was valid for both sexes, and some male students and teachers began wearing skirts to class. Conservative parents were furious. 'You can just imagine,' she said. The school had also hosted a commemoration of China's bloody Cultural Revolution, with activities that uncritically celebrated Mao's 'achievements'. Worst of all, the teachers belonged

to a communist-linked union and often went on strike, sometimes for months. A parents' group was formed to get the children back into the classroom, with little success. 'The Maoist and gay stuff was crazy, but we were able to deal with it,' she said. 'We couldn't get the union to budge.' She laughed bitterly and held open her hands. 'And so now we have the fascists.'

In situations like these Bolsonaro has deftly exploited conservative resentments. Under Rousseff, the government offended traditionalists by legalising same-sex marriage and designing materials for schools to combat homophobia. During the presidential race, Bolsonaro repeatedly told crowds that the PT had tried to introduce a 'gay kit' to their children. A rash of messages linked to his campaign arrived on voters' phones, accusing PT candidates of endorsing paedophilia.

For gay Brazilians these actions intensified a sense of siege. There has been an alarming increase in homophobic attacks. Brazil already had the world's highest levels of lethal violence against LGBTQ people, with 445 murders reported in 2017. During the presidential election some fifty attacks took place that were directly linked to Bolsonaro's supporters; among them were at least two incidents in which trans women were killed by men who invoked his name.

Some LGBTQ people are taking measures to protect themselves. In the Rio neighbourhood of Lapa, Halisson Paes, a 41-year-old lawyer, showed me the gym where he and his friends have been practising Krav Maga, the Israeli system of self-defence. 'It's not just aggression against the LGBTQ community,' Paes said, 'there's also more suicide. It's a toxic atmosphere.'

For Bolsonaro's supporters, rejecting gay rights is merely a return to common

sense. In January 2019 his human-rights ministry removed LGBTQ protections from its guidelines. At a press conference, the newly appointed minister, an evangelical pastor, declared, 'Girls will be princesses and boys will be princes. Girls wear pink, and boys wear blue.'

*

Bolsonaro's motto, repeated as an applause line at the end of speeches, is 'Brazil above everything, God above all'. Although he was raised Catholic he had himself baptised as an evangelical early in his campaign by being ceremonially dunked in the Jordan River. The influence of evangelical Christians has increased tremendously in Brazil, especially among poor and working-class people; as many as 30 per cent of Brazilians now regard themselves as evangelical, up from a minuscule number a few decades ago.

One morning I went to see Marcelo Crivella, the mayor of Rio de Janeiro and the country's most prominent evangelical politician. At sixty-two, Crivella has been an engineer, a gospel singer, a missionary in Africa, a federal senator and a minister of fisheries. He is also a bishop in the Universal Church of the Kingdom of God, a neo-Pentecostal sect with millions of followers (see 'Prosperity Now' on page 79). The church was founded in 1977 by Crivella's uncle, Edir Macedo, who has built it into a billion-dollar empire. Macedo's television network, RecordTV, is the third largest in Brazil, and his central church, a replica of Solomon's Temple

clad in stone shipped from Israel, towers eighteen storeys over São Paulo. Macedo threw his support behind Bolsonaro late in the presidential race. The final debate was held on Globo, Brazil's largest network. Bolsonaro, who refers to Globo as 'the enemy', skipped it to appear on RecordTV.

Crivella, casually dressed in slacks and a blue shirt, was disarmingly friendly, although two aides sat nearby filming our conversation. He told me that his political work was divinely inspired. 'Four thousand years ago the Bible told us that corruption is the root of all evil,' he said. He spoke of the far-ranging investigations undertaken by Judge Sérgio Moro. 'One manager alone received bribes of $100 million!' he exclaimed. 'It is because of this corruption that the Church has gained space.'

When Crivella looks at Bolsonaro, he told me, 'I see what half of Brazilians see – a bright future.' But many of the traits for which Bolsonaro is criticised – that he is a racist and a misogynist, that he distrusts indigenous people, that he thinks blacks are lazy – seem inconsistent with ecumenical Christian values. When I asked Crivella about it, he laughed and said, 'Like any other politician, Bolsonaro makes mistakes.' Then he quickly diverted the conversation. 'Talking about the blacks, I can tell you something,' he said. 'Brazil began with sugar cane, and sugar cane was the blacks. At the time of our grandfathers, Brazil was coffee, and coffee was the blacks. These people built the country, working more than any other people. Unfortunately, today – I would say because of our unequal society – three out of every four prison inmates are blacks.' Crivella assumed a sad expression. 'This is something that will be solved in time.'

In Brazil, questions of race are omnipresent. During the three centuries

Left: Avenida Paulista is one of the most important thoroughfares in São Paulo, home to many financial and cultural institutions. As a symbol of the city's economic and political power, it has been the focus of numerous political protests.

The Lula era will be remembered as the one in which Brazilian politics made use of communications and marketing to promote programmes for social inclusion that were criticised by the president's opponents as paternalistic. But Lula's instincts were correct: his success was down to the fact that for the first time a large section of the population who teetered on the poverty line were suddenly included in the political discourse. It seems symbolic that one of his first reforms, dating from 2003, was Luz para Todos, Light for All, an infrastructure revolution that brought electricity to remote and rural areas. The most powerful slogan of the whole campaign was Fome Zero, Zero Hunger, while the main programme was Bolsa Família, Family Allowance, a monthly cheque worth a few dozen reals, which represented the first time that thousands of people had ever received income in their lives, particularly in the North and Northeast regions, the poorest parts of the country – and where the president himself came from. The distribution of wealth provided a boost for the whole economy, also benefiting large insurers and banks, given the impetus provided to micro-credit. It could be said that as well as creating new citizens with new rights Lula saw an opportunity to create new consumers. On another front, his first government introduced a fundamental reform of access to education, particularly to universities. In 2004 it launched the Programa Universidade para Todos, University for All, allocating thousands of grants to low-income families and introducing quotas for black and ethnic-minority students, who had long been largely excluded from university education.

before Brazil abolished slavery in 1888, it imported almost five million Africans as slaves. Over time, escaped slaves carved out communities from the wilderness, which became known as *quilombos*. Lula and Dilma saw Brazilians of African descent as their constituents and made sure that the *quilombos* benefited from government programmes and from new infrastructure. Bolsonaro has long griped about such special dispensations. In a 2017 speech at Hebraica, a Jewish club in Rio, he described visiting a *quilombo*. 'The lightest African descendant weighed seven arrobas [105 kilograms/230 pounds]. They don't do anything. They don't serve even to procreate any more.'

Forty-five minutes from Bolsonaro's home town is a *quilombo* called Ivaporunduva. The road there runs through the forested Iguape River valley, past banana plantations, an Apostolic church named the Last Call and small farmhouses with red-tiled roofs. Ivaporunduva is a ramshackle farming community, built near the Devil's Cavern, a remote place where runaway slaves once hid from hunting parties.

Elson Alves da Silva, the *quilombo*'s leader, a bearded man in his thirties, told me that when he was a child he and most of his neighbours lived in wooden houses without electricity. Lula, in his first term, had carried out a programme called Luz para Todos, Light for All, bringing rural communities throughout Brazil on to the power grid. The PT had also backed a scholarship programme that enabled Silva to study history and education in São Paulo. He was now the headmaster of an elementary school in a neighbouring community. 'There was a time when the laws in Brazil said that "Negroes" and lepers couldn't attend school,' Silva told me. 'This is a legacy that is very real to us.'

During Bolsonaro's first days in office

1822

Independence from Portugal. Brazil becomes an empire and cuts its ties with the motherland. The crown of the constitutional monarchy is taken by Pedro I, succeeded in 1831 by his son Pedro II. Independence is commemorated every year on 7 September.

1888

Abolition of slavery, enacted by the so-called Lei Áurea, or Golden Law, on 13 May by the daughter of Emperor Pedro II, Dona Princesa Isabel.

1889

Proclamation of the republic after the abdication of Pedro II following the advance of republican movements that demand a constitution based on federal states.

1922

Modern Art Week in São Paolo. The first major international cultural event marking the rise to prominence of artists and writers who would go on to leave their mark on the first half of the 20th century and build Brazil's image as a modernist country.

1930

A coup d'état sweeps away the República Velha and triggers the Revolution of 1930, led by Getúlio Vargas. With an eye to Mussolini's regime in Italy and a populist attitude, Vargas governs by limiting political freedoms and freedom of expression, keeping hold on power, with a few interruptions, until 1954, when he commits suicide in the presidential palace.

1931

The statue of Christ the Redeemer is erected on the summit of Mount Corcovado, Rio de Janeiro. The project is designed by the French sculptor Paul Landowski (the face is created by the Romanian sculptor Gheorghe Leonida) and built by Brazilian engineer Heitor da Silva Costa in collaboration with a French colleague, Albert Caquot.

1950

The Jornalista Mário Filho Stadium, known as the Maracanã, is inaugurated on 16 June. It becomes Brazil's most important sporting venue but is also the scene of the *Seleção*'s first stunning defeat, at the hands of Uruguay, in the football World Cup of the same year.

1960

After only four years of construction work the capital is moved from Rio de Janeiro to Brasilia at the instigation of President Juscelino Kubitschek de Oliveira. A plateau in the interior was chosen as the site for a futuristic city, and the project awarded to the architect Oscar Niemeyer and the urban planner Lúcio Costa.

1964

A military coup forces President João Goulart to flee the country. The first military government is led by General Humberto de Alencar Castelo Branco, followed by Artur da Costa e Silva, who in 1968 is responsible for the Institutional Act Number 5, which tightened the grip of the dictatorship. The regime formally lasts until 1985, and a new republican constitution is signed in 1988.

1979

Signature on 28 August of the law granting amnesty for all political crimes on the part of the dictatorship as well as opponents of the regime. Those who had gone into exile are able to return home.

1989

First free elections following the end of the dictatorship. Fernando Collor de Mello is elected president but resigns just over two years later under threat of impeachment.

he signed a flurry of executive orders. One of them was a directive to cut back the Bolsa Família, Lula's food-assistance programme, which Silva said had helped save his community from destitution. Bolsonaro's new minister of agriculture, a representative of the agribusiness lobby, had advocated abolishing the *quilombos*' legal status. Silva said, 'Bolsonaro seems to believe certain groups don't belong and should be eliminated.'

*

In the farm town of Canarana in central Brazil, indigenous hunter-gatherers come to market to buy staples: tobacco, rice, medicine. On the way, they pass Cargill grain silos and a John Deere dealership that sells tractors to commercial farms in the area. Towns like this mark a political fault line. In the Brazilian interior, a vast area with few roads or railways, the battles for land and survival among settlers, miners, ranchers and indigenous groups recall life on the early American frontier.

Indigenous rights and environmental policy are intertwined in Brazil: most of its indigenous territories, about an eighth of the country's total area, are located in the Amazon, whose rainforest generates 20 per cent of the world's oxygen. Under Lula, the government constrained commercial activity in the region, reducing deforestation by more than 70 per cent. Although Rousseff's administration rolled back some foresting regulations during the recession, Brazil remained a leader in climate-change policy.

Bolsonaro views environmental protections as a senseless brake on development. He has vowed to withdraw from the Paris Agreement, and he dismisses environmental groups as Marxists and elitists, who have co-opted indigenous leaders to serve international interests. In his first week in office, he tweeted about the Amazon region: 'Less than one million people live in those places isolated from the real Brazil. They are exploited and manipulated by NGOs. Together let's integrate those citizens and give value to all Brazilians.' The head of Aprosoja, Brazil's grain growers' association, said approvingly, 'Indians want to be productive, too.' During the three-month presidential campaign season, deforestation surged by 50 per cent.

I went to Canarana to visit the Xavante, one of the country's 305 tribal groups. I arrived at noon, after a 22-hour bus ride from Brasilia. Since daybreak, all I had seen were soya fields, most of them reportedly owned by Blairo Maggi, Brazil's 'Soya King', who once won Greenpeace's Golden Chainsaw Award for the huge tracts of wilderness he was responsible for destroying. Three Xavante were waiting for me at a little bus station – burly men with long black hair and wooden plugs in their earlobes. Their leader was Jamiro, a friendly man in his thirties who spoke Portuguese. We filled their car with provisions and headed off.

The Xavante are hunter-gatherers who once lived in the rolling low jungle of Goiás state, where Brasilia is now situated. After the Portuguese conquistadores enslaved them in the 18th century, they fled to the western state of Mato Grosso. In the 1960s white ranchers began moving in on their land, and conflict ensued, until in 1977 the government declared their territory a federal reserve. They ended up with eight disconnected tracts, spread out over several hundred miles – islets of wilderness surrounded by what is now a Kansas-size expanse of industrial farms.

For decades Brazil's indigenous-affairs agency, FUNAI, limited farming and mining in indigenous territories by creating reserves that were off limits to developers.

'"When he was stabbed, he said, 'God saved me.' But it was not God who saved him. It was the Devil."'

Within days of taking office Bolsonaro transferred control of FUNAI to a newly created ministry led by Damares Alves, an ultra-conservative evangelical pastor. The power to set aside reserves was given to the agriculture ministry, overseen by Tereza Cristina Dias, the former leader of the congressional farm caucus. Marina Silva, a prominent environmentalist and former legislator, told me that these actions evoked the influx of settlement that devastated Native Americans in the USA. 'The introduction of the American model in Brazil could have the same effect here as it did there, of dividing the indigenous groups and fragmenting their populations.'

Bolsonaro's environmental policy is overseen by Ricardo Salles, a libertarian lawyer who recently spent a year as the environment secretary for São Paulo state. In Brasilia, he suggested to me that FUNAI had been holding indigenous people back. 'The Indians are not considered responsible for their own actions and are treated as second-class citizens. They are used by government officials. They can't decide about anything!' Salles said. 'We must decide whether they should be treated as second-class people or are citizens like us and have the right to cultivate the area for agriculture or to give some of their lands over to mining and infrastructure, so as to secure some gains for themselves.' Salles's plan to protect the Amazon forest from illegal development was to deploy aerial technology, to provide 'real-time surveillance of what is going on, so we can act quickly'.

Two hours outside Canarana, the soya fields gave way to bush, and Jamiro explained that we had entered the reservation. The Xavante village of Etenhiritipá consisted of a half-circle of family huts made of palm leaves and sticks, set around an expanse of grass and dirt dotted with shade trees. In the distance stood the Serra do Roncador mountains, and beyond them lay the Rio das Mortes – the River of Death.

Every day at sunset, the young men of Etenhiritipá gather in the centre of the village, which they call the Circle, and begin an evening ritual, chanting and stomping their feet. In a ceremony during my visit they paused the chanting so that the older men could speak. Jamiro moved to the centre of the Circle, carrying a 'talking stick', a short club that conveyed the right to speak. 'We are worried about our reserve – the reserve of the indigenous people,' he said. 'Without the reserves there is no air. So our concern is not just about us. It's about everyone.' Jamiro directed himself as if to Bolsonaro. 'You have to think better, Jair.' Turning to the men of the Circle, Jamiro said, 'When he was stabbed, he said, "God saved me." But it was not God who saved him. It was the Devil that saved him. And the other one, too. What's his name, the one with the white hair?'

Several men called out 'Trupi!' – their name for Trump.

Jamiro nodded. 'That's the one,' he said. He referred again to Bolsonaro. 'He does not respect nature,' he said. 'God created nature. That is how he sends us our food. We have to take care of nature. If nature is finished off, everything is going to burst.'

*

In March 2019, while Brazil was celebrating *carnaval*, Bolsonaro posted a video

Fernando Henrique Cardoso

Born in Rio de Janeiro in 1931, elected for
the first time in 1995 and for a second term
in 1999, Cardoso remained in office until the
end of his term in 2003. A sociology professor
and political scientist, he started out as a
social democrat and was elected under the
banner of the centrist, social-democratic PSDB
(Partido da Social Democracia Brasileira), a
party strongly rooted in the city of São Paulo.
His government continued the Plano Real, the
economic stabilisation measures begun under
the previous presidency but also undertook neo-
liberal reforms such as the vast privatisations
of strategic state enterprises. His government
also established a number of social programmes
later taken up by his successor, Lula.

Luiz Inácio Lula da Silva, aka 'Lula'

Born in 1945 in Caetés, Lula had a trade-unionist
background in the metal-working sector before
being elected for the first time in 2002 for the left-
wing PT (Partido dos Trabalhadores, the Workers'
Party), of which he was a founding member. His
government was marked by an unprecedented
economic boom with strong growth indicators
and a complete renewal of the country's image
on the international stage, but it also suffered
corruption scandals, starting with the so-called
Mensalão Scandal (deriving from the Portuguese
for 'monthly payment'), which saw many
government figures and members of parliament
accused of buying and selling parliamentary
votes. However, Lula managed to come back from
this and rebuild both his own image and that of
the government and was re-elected in 2006.

Dilma Rousseff

Born in Belo Horizonte in 1947 to a family with Bulgarian roots, Rousseff was a left-wing militant in her youth and took part in the struggle against the dictatorship, which even led to her imprisonment and torture. She later pursued a career as a civil servant. As a member of the PT she joined Lula's second government, serving in ministerial posts, and was chosen by Lula as his successor to continue the party's political project. She was elected in 2010, becoming Brazil's first woman president, and ran a successful re-election campaign in 2014, but support for her fell drastically during her second term, partly as a result of Brazil's severe economic crisis and street protests following revelations of government corruption. On 31 August 2016 she stepped down from the presidency following an impeachment trial.

Michel Temer

Born in 1940 to Lebanese immigrants who had settled in the town of Tietê in São Paolo state, after a career as a lawyer and public prosecutor, Temer took part in the post-dictatorship constituent assembly and won a parliamentary seat in the 1990s for the progressive PMDB (Partido do Movimento Democrático Brasileiro, the Brazilian Democratic Movement Party). He held high-level posts, including the presidency of the Chamber of Deputies. An experienced political communicator and a dominant figure in the party allied to Dilma Rousseff's candidacy in 2010, Temer served as vice-president during Rousseff's first term and was reconfirmed in the second. During her impeachment, in May 2016 Temer took over as president of the republic, passing a series of free-market economic reforms.

"'Brazil and the United States stand side by side in their efforts to ensure liberties and respect to traditional family lifestyles, respect to God, our Creator, against the gender ideology or the politically correct attitudes and against fake news.'"

on social media in which two men gave an ad-lib demonstration of sexual kink before a cheering crowd. 'I do not feel comfortable showing this, but ... this is what many of the street parties in Brazil's carnival have turned into,' he wrote. Internet searches for 'golden showers' spiked in Brazil. Critics rushed to argue that posting sex videos online, even by way of negative example, was not presidential behaviour. Others noted that the scene was not representative of *carnaval*, which in 2019 was distinguished mostly by protests against Bolsonaro. The samba school that was judged the best in the parade presented a retelling of Brazilian history from the perspective of black citizens and indigenous people. It also paid tribute to Marielle Franco, the councilwoman who was killed in 2018. In a subsequent Women's Day march, protesters gathered in nine cities to commemorate Franco's death and to condemn Bolsonaro's statements about women. On the day of the march, he claimed that his cabinet had reached gender parity, 'for the first time ever'. In fact, only two of the twenty-two posts were filled by women, a discrepancy that he explained by saying, 'Each woman here is worth ten men.' A boisterous *carnaval* chant – 'Hey, Bolsonaro, go fuck yourself' – spread to demonstrations across Brazil.

Even Bolsonaro's old friend Alberto Fraga was concerned that he was too divisive. Social media had helped him get elected, but, Fraga said, 'it's no way to run a country'. He was also worried about Bolsonaro's sons. 'His kids are too close,

too involved,' he said. Last month, amid allegations of campaign-finance fraud in Bolsonaro's party, Carlos accused a senior cabinet minister, Gustavo Bebianno, of lying to protect himself. Bebianno, who denied any wrongdoing, was soon fired. Flávio is being investigated in connection with luxury apartments that he purchased in Rio. The inquiry into Franco's killing has produced two new suspects, both former policemen. One lives in the same gated community as Bolsonaro and has a daughter who once dated Bolsonaro's youngest son. The other has been photographed greeting Bolsonaro with a friendly embrace. (Bolsonaro denies connections to either, saying that he has hugged thousands of policemen and that his son 'dated every girl in the community'.)

Bolsonaro's vice-president also presents a challenge. Mourão is not a long-time ally; he joined Bolsonaro's campaign just hours before the deadline for naming a running mate. A watchful, carefully spoken man of indigenous descent, Mourão entered the Black Needles academy in 1972, around the same time as Bolsonaro. Unlike his boss he stayed in the military for forty-six years, retiring in 2018 as a four-star general.

When I met Mourão in Brasilia, he shared the president's enthusiasm about working with the United States. 'There is great alignment between Mr Bolsonaro and Mr Trump, so I think that for the first time in years we have a government in Brazil that is pro-US,' he said. But when I asked whether the USA might build a military base in Brazil, as Bolsonaro has

Above: A fisherman on Ipanema beach, Rio de Janeiro.
Below: A cowboy in the city of Piracicaba, São Paulo state.

Order and Progress?

Above: São Paulo, a city with a rich architectural tradition; iconic landmarks include the neo-gothic cathedral, the Martinelli tower built in 1929 and Oscar Niemeyer's Edifício Copan. The colonial-style Pátio do Colégio church marks the spot where the city was founded by Jesuit priests in 1554.
Below: Ipanema beach, Rio de Janeiro, is known for its social life. Two mountains, the Dois Irmãos, the Two Brothers, stand at the western end of the beach, which is divided into sections demarcated by lifeguard posts.

suggested, he demurred. 'That won't happen,' he said. 'We don't need another army in our country.'

Mourão often gently contradicts Bolsonaro's positions. When Bolsonaro celebrated the news that his rival Jean Wyllys was afraid to return to Brazil, Mourão said, 'Anyone who threatens a congressman is committing a crime against democracy.' In January 2019 Bolsonaro attended the World Economic Forum in Davos, and Mourão became acting president for four days. In that time he announced that Brazil had no immediate plans to move its embassy in Israel to Jerusalem and that he didn't believe increased access to guns would reduce violence. When I asked Mourão about his differences with Bolsonaro, he replied judiciously, 'We each have our ideas. But from the moment he expresses his, his idea will be mine. If I didn't express my point of view, I wouldn't be loyal.'

Still, his independence rankles some of Bolsonaro's allies. In November 2018 Carlos Bolsonaro tweeted: 'It's not just Jair Bolsonaro's enemies but also those closest to him who have an interest in his death' – a message widely understood to have been aimed at Mourão. Bannon referred to him as 'useless and unpleasant'. Gerald Brant, a New York-based hedge-fund executive and a friend of the Bolsonaros, told me, 'Everyone is pissed off at Mourão, who has turned out to be a real pain in the ass as well as a media hog. The problem is, he can't be gotten rid of, since he's an elected official.'

When I asked Mourão about his ambitions as vice-president, he said, 'I would like to head a new government centre, so we can control the big projects, oversee what the ministries are doing. I would spare the president a lot of problems.'

'Has Bolsonaro agreed to this?' I asked.

Mourão gave a non-committal nod. 'He is thinking about it,' he said.

*

In March 2019 Bolsonaro flew to Washington, DC, to visit Trump. For Bolsonaro the trip was a respite from the squabbles in Brazil, where his approval rating has slid to 34 per cent. He and Trump traded personalised soccer jerseys and congratulated each other on their successful campaigns. At Trump International Hotel, Bannon and Brant hosted a screening of *The Garden of Afflictions*, a documentary about the philosopher Olavo de Carvalho; Eduardo Bolsonaro arrived wearing a cap that read 'Make Brazil Great Again'. Afterwards Brant said, 'It's stunning how two sides can be so on board with ideas, values, policies – stunning.'

At a press conference in the Rose Garden, Trump said that he and Bolsonaro had 'discussed the strong economic ties between our nations, grounded in the principles of fairness and reciprocity. My favourite word: reciprocity.' There were new commitments concerning agribusiness and the sale of beef. Trump announced that he would designate Brazil a 'major non-NATO ally – or even, possibly, if you start thinking about it, maybe a NATO ally'. The designation would facilitate military cooperation and give Bolsonaro easier access to US weapons.

Trump had covered beef and bullets – two of the 'Three Bs' that help define Brazilian politics. Bolsonaro summoned the third, the Bible. 'Brazil and the United States stand side by side in their efforts to ensure liberties and respect to traditional family lifestyles, respect to God, our Creator, against the gender ideology or the politically correct attitudes and against fake news.' Trump smiled. ✒

Funk, Pride and Prejudice

Coarse, over the top and foul-mouthed but also pioneering, liberating and feminist, Brazil's *funkeiras* are turning the tables on a patriarchal society only interested in perfectly sculpted female bodies and fighting against the stereotype of white middle-class beauty.

ALBERTO RIVA
Translated by Alan Thawley

Left: The singer Carolina de Oliveiro Lourenço, aka MC Carol, famous for her lyrics that deal with social issues and make use of sexually explicit double entendres.

'My man is a fool fit only to wash my panties,' sings the *funkeira*. 'If you complain,' she warns him, 'I'll send you to the kitchen to do the dishes, too. Not happy with that? I'll have you sleeping outside the front door, because I want to go out and have fun.'

People say she's coarse, over the top and foul-mouthed, but perhaps MC Carol, one of the biggest black female funk stars in Brazil, is just subverting the rules, turning the picture on its head to see what happens – starting with herself and her own body. On stage for the TV show *Furacão 2000*, in front of a dance floor the size of a football pitch, MC Carol looms large in her lemon-yellow wedge heels, her curves overflowing her denim shorts, jiggling under her skin-tight bodysuit. She stands in the middle of the stage and brings the microphone to her lips. Rather than singing, she shouts the words. 'I want air conditioning, couldn't give a shit about a fan, it's hot as hell! Fuck me with your frozen dick! And if the air conditioner breaks, I'll find myself another man.' If the girl from Ipanema was a wave flowing light as the breeze on the golden sand, the *funkeira* stands on stage with her legs planted like two cannon. She has no interest in conforming to the prevailing ideal of beauty. She wants power, the power that has been denied her.

Along with other similar black female artists who come from the *favela*, MC Carol is part of a musical movement that encapsulates one of the strongest driving forces in Brazil today: a new awareness of the female role in the lowest stratum of society. It is in this very large but neglected section of the population that social roles, both within the family and in terms of gender relations, have remained rigid, almost unchanged for decades – in fact, for more than a century. You could say that until recent years they had remained in place since colonial times.

In music the wave is growing. At one time women's funk could be seen only at Saturday evening parties on the outskirts of the city, far from the centre, like Nova Iguaçu and São Gonçalo, but now it has invaded YouTube and the nightspots of Copacabana. Funk is still a predominantly carioca phenomenon – that is, based in and native to Rio – although it has gone on to inspire artists from the rest of Brazil as well.

MC Carol is not alone. The list of her peers is long and includes such artists

ALBERTO RIVA is an Italian writer and journalist who has lived in Rio de Janeiro. His books include the novel *Sete* (Mondadori, 2011) and his exploration of Rio, *Seguire i pappagalli fino alla fine* (Il Saggiatore, 2008). Music is one of his great passions, and he has written several books on the subject, including *Note necessarie* (Minimum Fax, 2004) with Enrico Rava, *Parliamo di musica* and *Il monello, il guru, l'alchimista* with Stefano Bollani, both published by Mondadori (2013, 2015). He also writes for *Il Venerdì di Repubblica* and *Internazionale*.

as Jojo Todynho, MC Mayara, Ludmilla, MC Rebecca and the rapper Karol Conka. People call them feminists, and they embrace this – they are, after all, singing from a female perspective and expressing women's resistance in one of the world's most male-chauvinist societies.

In the case of MC Carol and Jojo Todynho, they do so while proudly displaying their queen-sized bodies, deliberately countering the stereotype of white, sculpted, gym-honed beauty of middle-class girls jogging on Ipanema beach at sunset. But they also express their attitude in another way: using satire, profanity and hyperbole to challenge established modes of behaviour. And sex, precisely because it is an instrument of oppression, plays an important role. In one of her most frequently played but also widely criticised songs, MC Carol asks, 'What's up, dear? What's wrong, my love? I've just started and you've already come? Let's face it, you fucked me really badly.' But we should not fall into the trap of thinking that MC Carol is simply someone with a talent for being provocative who strings together a few colourful lines full of double entendres (perhaps not so double) to drive an increasingly diverse crowd wild simply because that is what her audience likes. It's true that she started out that way, playing the sex card and subverting roles, but sex is a subject for which all these artists have gone into battle. 'Cai de Boca' ('Use Your Mouth') is MC Rebecca's ode to oral sex, which she suggests is something men should do for women without having to be asked. Cunnilingus is a must. 'Lalá', one of Karol Conka's hits, is devoted to the subject, the title enunciated and repeated while explicitly miming the action with her tongue. 'Now you're crying, you're only complaining because I had you on your knees giving me *lalá* for a few hours ...' she raps, going on to say that 'they talk and talk and then don't know the difference between a clitoris and an ovary'.

IT DIDN'T HAPPEN OVERNIGHT

It all began with funk – but we're not talking Funkadelic and Kool and the Gang. Funk carioca has nothing to do with that rhythmic groove and its irresistible tunes, the raunchiness of James Brown or the bass of Sly and the Family Stone. Funk carioca is a stripped-back, repetitive rhythm, a metallic, synthesised mantra, an echoing, hammering beat over which the voice, shouting into the microphone crushed against the singer's lips, reels off lines that don't necessarily rhyme – and aren't always lines as such.

It landed in Rio in the early 1970s at big parties that were still infused with African-American soul, such as the notorious baile put on by DJ BigBoy. They took place in outlying districts of the city and could attract crowds of up to ten thousand people. Then the music changed. Taking cues from Miami bass, the melodies dried up and were stripped back to reveal naked, raw beats. These so-called 'bases' were in great demand, the goal being to find the right base to pair with the unaccompanied vocals, which were shouted, rhythmic and sometimes rhymed. Drums were replaced by the sampler. It wasn't funky any more. From its origins as entertainment, Rio's funk went through a period marked by violence, when events could end up as battles between opposing factions at which people could – and did – lose their lives.

Then something changed again, as funk re-emerged as a characteristic expression of the *comunidade*, of the *favela*, in the hands of spontaneous artists who discovered they could make use of these bases as backing tracks for songs

PROIBIDÃO: FORBIDDEN FUNK

With similarities to US gangsta rap, funk proibidão, forbidden funk, emerged in the 1990s in many of Rio's *favelas* as a genre with lyrics that described with marked realism the world from which the music emanated, the battles between narcos and police, and for this reason the artists often faced the accusation that they were apologists for narcotraffickers. Certain exponents of the hardest forms of funk, who later became nationally famous – the rapper and social activist MV Bill, for example – have always rejected the accusation, explaining that the music is a raw and unadorned reflection of reality rather than an apology. The subject matter is controversial, covering: the codes imposed by Rio's various drug-trafficking factions, like the Comando Vermelho, the Terceiro Comando and Amigos dos Amigos; a meticulous description of criminal attitudes, such as the vendetta against so-called X9s, the 'traitors' who inform and spy – a label that terrifies people in the *favela* – and the no-holds-barred description of the executions and punishments they face; plus various types of weapons and what they are used for. Funk proibidão has sometimes also been accused of using a coded language to send messages to enemies or accomplices. By extension, although they should be seen as different styles and genres, songs about drugs have also attracted the 'forbidden' label and the artists accused of being apologists for drug use. Overly explicit sex has been lumped into the same category, too, as in the case of Mr Catra.

about their reality and their stories. As a result, funk entered a lengthy period of quarantine and discrimination, born of poverty, as the two went hand in hand. *Favela* meant poverty; funk meant marginalised music made by people living on the margins. As an expression of the *favela*, to find space beyond the *favela* funk had to fight against a barrier that is not cultural but resides in the very structure of a society that the sociologist Jessé Souza defines as 'slavocratic', in other words, perpetuating the structure of colonial society in which a black person is a sub-citizen. This is where the violence (often police violence) originates and why perpetrators act with impunity, because black people in Brazil, according to Souza, 'are still slaves on the run from the plantation'. Of the 57,000 people murdered in Brazil in 2018, a significant majority was black. It is not easy to explain the extent to which the *favela* still remains a world apart from Brazil's middle-class society, but this prevailing climate of impunity could be a good indicator.

Well away from the cultural mainstream, funk developed as an outcast form of expression, born in the *favela* for the *favela*, and produced the phenomenon of the MCs known as *funkeiros* and their subject matter: violence in the community, drug trafficking and sex, a lot of sex, large amounts of sex. Observed, described and imposed from a male perspective. Take Mr Catra, a legendary figure in the sexualised funk proibidão scene of the 1990s and 2000s (how could we forget his hugely popular hit 'Uma Mamada de Manhã'

['Blow in the Morning'], which managed to combine references to marijuana and oral sex in a single phrase), who died before even reaching his fifties after a life of excess. Other artists who emerged in the same period were the pioneers of funk sensual, those who came from humble jobs and discovered they could be musicians, like Deize Tigrona and Tati Quebra-Barraca or groups like Bonde Faz Gostoso and Gaiola das Popozudas (former member Valesca Popozuda remains popular today). They all started singing about sex and girls' desires. So the first *funkeiras* landed on Planet Sex to take back a space that had been the exclusive preserve of male funk. Deize, who came from Cidade de Deus, the mega-*favela* immortalised in the 2002 film *City of God*, was the first to drop explicit lyrics that made use of double entendres, as in one song in which a doctor needs to give her an injection, and she sighs, 'It's burning, but it's going in …' A song by Bonde Faz Gostoso (the Gang that Does It Well) encouraged girls to visit the gynaecologist and not to neglect their bodies, proclaiming, 'We're in control.' The rallying cry was 'Let loose and talk about it!' Today's feminist funk would not exist without the funk sensual movement of fifteen years earlier, without that first spotlight turned on an expression of women's desires. They were ostracised because they were black women from the *favela*, and the reaction was an attempt to delegitimise their outburst. They were labelled pornographic, stigmatised and written off as little more than trash.

On the other hand, there was no feminist consciousness in that first phase of funk sensual: the message of the *funkeiras* was intrinsically feminist, but they rejected the label. In Denise Garcia's documentary on the era, its title taken from one of Tati's first hits, 'Sou

"'I'm independent, I don't accept impositions, keep your voice down, keep your hands down!'"

Feia Mas Tô na Moda' ('I'm Ugly But I'm in Fashion'), a notable figure in the movement, DJ Marlboro, explained it well: 'She was a feminist without carrying the card. Life taught her to be a feminist.'

SELF-PROCLAIMED FEMINISTS

Today things are different. For artists like MC Carol, tackling these subjects and positioning themselves on this battleground may well have begun as a way to earn some money, but it soon became something serious, the first step towards being part of something greater. It was no coincidence that MC Carol ended up meeting Karol Conka and working with her on a song that symbolises the movement, '100% Feminista', with its lyrics that read like a manifesto: 'I'm a woman, I'm black, my hair is curly ...' 'I'm independent, I don't accept impositions, keep your voice down, keep your hands down!' 'In my family I saw the woman with swollen eyes, beaten every day.' 'They told us we were inadequate. I don't agree! If you want to be heard, you need to shout louder.' MC Carol, who has reported being attacked and receiving death threats from her former partner, followed a clear path when she moved on from entertainment in a funk sensual style to feminist militancy, taking an explicit position of resistance that had specific political connotations.

Carolina de Oliveira Lourenço, aka MC Carol, was born in 1993 in Niterói, the city on the other side of Guanabara Bay from Rio that is home to the Contemporary Art Museum designed by Oscar Niemeyer. But she grew up in the Preventório *favela*, far from the tourist beauty spots. She says she became a *funkeira* by chance, getting

started after being pushed on to the stage. Even if that was how it happened, she immediately carved out a role for herself, mixing *putaria* material (sex and profanity) with more sophisticated output. She wrote a song based on her personal version of the history of Brazil 'Não Foi Cabral' ('It Wasn't Cabral'), which begins with a parody of the Brazilian national anthem and goes on to list the crimes committed by the colonisers. One of her first songs, 'Bateu Uma Onda Forte' ('It Kicked Hard'), became a slogan for the demonstrations against the rise in fare prices on public transport in São Paolo in 2016. Even though she's conscious of her vocation as a pop star (she also took part in a Fox reality show, which confirmed her status as an icon), MC Carol naturally ended up aligning herself with the demands of Brazil's new feminism: why should a woman like her still be required to assert her independence every day, and why should she not consider herself beautiful, sexy even, without being reduced to a mere sex object?

After the murder of the city councillor Marielle Franco and her driver in Rio on 14 March 2018, the first political assassination in Brazil since the return of democracy in 1985, MC Carol devoted a song to her in which she sings, 'I feel imprisoned and demoralised, they killed me in that car as well. I feel hate, fear, terror, slavery is not over, they are killing black people, tired of being mistreated, robbed, oppressed, arrested, framed ...'

MARIA'S LAW

Anyone questioning whether taking such a strong stance is necessary can check the numbers. Gender-based violence is a scourge on Brazilian society. According to Rio's Institute of Public Safety, 350 cases of femicide were reported in 2018 in Rio state alone, along with 288 cases of attempted femicide. Of these crimes, 62 per cent were committed in the home, with 56 per cent committed by partners or ex-partners. Every twenty-four hours four women suffer physical injuries and the same number are threatened. According to data gathered by *O Globo* for the whole of Brazil over the period 2016–18, there were twelve thousand cases of femicide and 900,000 women applied to a judge to be placed under protection.

The fight against the phenomenon is based on two pieces of legislation: the Femicide Law, enacted in 2018, and the Maria da Penha Law, dating from 2006. The latter takes its name from an appalling case, that of Maria da Penha Maia Fernandes, a pharmacist born in 1945 in the city of Fortaleza, the state capital of Ceará. In 1983 she survived two murder attempts at the hands of her husband, a university lecturer originally from Colombia. On the first occasion he shot her in the back while she was asleep in an attempt to make it look like a robbery. She lost the use of her legs. Four months later, after she came out of hospital, he kidnapped her for fifteen days and tried to electrocute her while she was taking a bath.

The court case dragged on for many years before a sentence was handed down, but her ex-husband still managed to avoid prison. In 1998 the case ended up before the Inter-American Commission on Human Rights (IACHR/OAS), which accused Brazil of a serious omission given the violence she had suffered. In 2002, in the absence of an adequate response from the Brazilian institutions, taking this one case as their starting point, a consortium of NGOs began to outline a legislative plan that would fill the gap – or rather, the abyss – that Maria and women like her were destined to fall into. That same year, thanks to pressure from the international body, her ex-husband went to prison, nineteen years after the crimes had been committed – but for less than three years.

On 7 August 2006 President Lula approved the Maria da Penha Law (Federal Law 11340), named for the central figure in this unequal struggle, who went from being an anonymous pharmacist to one of the leading experts and activists in the fight against gender-based violence in South America. The law was regarded as innovative by the UN because in addition to physical violence it included psychological, moral and sexual violence as well as violence against property. Although the figures for gender-based violence in Brazil remain high, it is estimated that the law has helped to reduce attacks by 10 per cent.

COMING TO TERMS WITH THE PAST

Brazil is a country that has struggled to come to terms with women's rights. The first state to allow women to vote was Rio Grande do Norte in 1927. It wasn't until 1934 that a federal law was extended countrywide, and a woman, the writer and doctor Carlota Pereira de Queirós, entered parliament. But she and the other pioneers of women's civil rights all had one thing in common: they were white.

So what about black women? Even though the law that enshrined the end of slavery dates from 1888, black women have continued to feel the symbolic weight of the chains, the discriminatory rules of the *casa grande* – the plantation owner's residence – which stood some considerable distance from the *senzala*, the slave

THE PASSENGER   Alberto Riva

quarters. An example of these virtual chains? Even in 2016 one of the most prestigious sports clubs in Rio de Janeiro displayed a sign prohibiting children's nannies from using the same bathroom as the members, inviting the *babás*, inevitably black women in white uniforms, to use the children's bathrooms. A truly classic case of apartheid well into the 21st century in a country that, curiously, has built its national identity on the myth of the so-called 'cordial man', arising from peaceful coexistence between the 'three sad races': the colonisers, the slaves and the colonised. A grand illusion. (See 'The Cordial Man' on page 71.)

Women have played the most difficult role in this story, particularly black women – that huge population of workers who every morning leave Rio's vast slums, such as Rocinha, Vidigal, Dona Marta, Providência, Cabrito and Coroa or come down from the Complexo da Maré (which is not a hill but an endless expanse of uneven ground), as Marielle Franco did, and spread across the city to work. As a result, the characteristics that were once causes of discrimination (and still are) for MC Carol have now become a proud calling card: she's happy to describe herself as 'fat, black and *favelada*'.

Despite what we might think, music has not always been an entirely positive force in this difficult struggle. Samba is the form of music that more than any other provided Brazilians with entertainment over the course of the 20th century, told their stories, defined them and, paradoxically, united them. Yet it often, if not always, perpetuated some of the most harmful stereotypes. Not so much in terms of its function as a realistic 'chronicle' but through its male perspective on the female world.

A very well-known samba from the 1940s, sung by Jorge Veiga with his trademark swing, included the lyric 'Oh that woman, always in a bad mood, would anyone want to take her?' Bezerra da Silva, another samba artist, railed against the figure of the *mulher que engana* (cheating woman). In his lyrics we are told she deserves to be 'thrown into a colony, her ears cut off, her head shaved, to carry rocks to show the extent of her disgrace', a sentiment not so far removed from the lyrics of today's *funkeiros* like MC Denny – the author of such lines as 'if you ask me to stop I won't stop' – who has been accused of encouraging rape and has been banned from digital platforms, something that has also happened to other MCs expressing similar sentiments.

'I NEVER WANTED PITY!'

And yet it was out of the samba scene, from its rules and its culture, that a pioneering figure of female resistance emerged in the 1950s, a woman who was undoubtedly the inspiration for today's female Brazilian artists, black or otherwise. Elza Soares, born in 1930, is still at the heart of Brazilian music. In 2018, backed by a crop of young female composers and songwriters, she called one of her albums *Deus É Mulher*, 'God Is a Woman'. Although she came from a samba background, Soares was not afraid to rap on other people's songs, for instance Caetano Veloso's 'Haiti', one of the Bahia-born composer's most anti-racist songs. And even in her most recent work, in which she tackles the subjects of sex, discrimination and violence against the black population, Elza Soares still chants each word in her husky voice as if it were a slogan. 'I pay a lot of attention to the words, the message, what my songs say,' she explains. 'At the moment it's important to me to talk about the situation that Brazil is going through, to talk about black people, women, the gay community, which suffers so much through the cowardice of people who discriminate. This is my world, this is what my work is about. You have to look reality in the face.' For Elza the feminist struggle played a decisive role. 'Today I can see people are more sensitive, more combative, more aware, women are more informed than they once were and take better care of themselves. Women today have more space to speak, to react.' Born into a very poor community on the outskirts of Rio, Elza began by helping her mother, a laundrywoman, and had her first children while still under age. 'I got married and became a mother very young,' she says. 'As a teenager I was already an adult. I had to be. My life has always been difficult. I was a poor child from a poor family, but I never wanted pity, never! I always had character. From the outset I wanted to help my mother and father because it wasn't easy for them. I worked so hard from when I was a little girl. But I never wanted people to feel sorry for me or think "poor Elza"! Elza was a child who wanted to win: there was a road ahead of her, and so let's go down it, she thought!'

And that's exactly what she did. She became famous in the 1960s and was the first to bring swing, shades of the blues and the sophistication of jazz to samba singing. She was beautiful as well. The great footballer Garrincha fell for her and she for him. Unfortunately, he already had a wife and a brood of children, whom he abandoned but returned to periodically. Everyone blamed Elza, though. The prevailing moralism and the newspapers singled her out as the source of the misery suffered by the bandy-legged champion, the dribbling prodigy who drank like a fish, so much so that he died a penniless alcoholic, alone in the world, at the age of forty-nine. Elza bore him a son, who died

#ELENÃO

On 29 September 2018, at the culmination of the presidential election campaign (the first round of voting took place a week later), a major demonstration was held in a large public square in São Paulo known as Largo da Batata, having been announced on the Facebook page of a group calling itself Mulheres Unidas Contra Bolsonaro, Women United Against Bolsonaro. In the space of a few weeks the page exceeded a million hits, then at the beginning of that month the hashtag #EleNão was created, effectively summing up the movement's rallying cry: Not Him. What was new was that this was a manifestly female public demonstration, an uprising driven by women. The goal was to express their rejection of the racist, sexist, authoritarian and homophobic views that the presidential candidate was expressing in an increasingly brazen fashion. Similar demonstrations were held in all the major Brazilian cities and internationally, including in London and New York. The movement also attracted Brazilian stars such as the actress Sônia Braga, the singer Daniela Mercury and the composer Maria Gadu as well as international stars like Madonna.

as a child. Garrincha ran his car off the road while he was drunk, killing Elza's mother. In a bid to stop him drinking she vowed to cut off all her hair, and she kept that promise. Reappearing in a monumental Afro wig, she returned to the stage having been kept away, following anonymous threats, during the darkest period of the military dictatorship. Why was she targeted? Because she was a free woman. Worse, she was free, black and had been born into poverty but had managed to escape.

A woman of many struggles, Elza always said she felt the double weight of being black and a woman. She was already getting old when she sang the beautiful protest song 'A Carne': 'The cheapest meat on the market is black meat.'

When we see the emergence of stars like MC Carol and her feminist funk colleagues in Brazil, the spirit of Elza Soares is always in the background. What's new is that once they also had to be traditionally beautiful, as she was; today that is no longer a requirement: *sou feia mas tô na moda*.

NOT JUST FASHION
Jojo Todynho, real name Jordana Gleise de Jesus Menezes, was born not far from Niterói, in Bangu, where, far from the sea and the picture-postcard views, Rio peters out into an endless suburb known as the Baixada Fluminense. At twenty-two she made a name for herself on social media talking about men – or rather, her independence from men. In one of her videos she says, 'We don't need to bring men home. You want to fuck? Then pay for a motel! We don't live on dick alone: I live on food, water, being able to pay for my luxuries.' She has a turbulent relationship with her fans. Sometimes she responds in her videos to certain comments – a polemical spirit who easily flies off the handle. The

Right and pages 46–7: The dancers who accompany MC Carol during her performances.

hit video that propelled her to fame, 'Que Tiro Foi Esse' ('What a Shot that Was' – with all that implies) was nothing short of a deconstruction of sexual preconceptions. Jojo dominates the screen with her larger-than-life assets, displayed to eye-popping effect. Her funk has more of a Beyoncé feel to it – in fact, Beyoncé is a legendary figure to almost all the *funkeiras* looking to overturn the marginal role allotted to them by society.

Funk today is emerging from its 'pure' phase, with melody and pop making rapid inroads. One example is Ludmilla Oliveira da Silva, now known simply as Ludmilla, although at the beginning of her career a few years back she actually arrived on the scene under the pseudonym of MC Beyoncé. She grew up in the suburb of Duque de Caxias, which is still part of Rio de Janeiro, although if you did happen to visit you'd feel a long, long way from Sugarloaf Mountain. She was another singer who posted her first songs on YouTube. With its imperious tone, 'Fala Mal de Mim' ('Badmouth Me') notched up a million views. Ludmilla then signed to a major label and built a career out of polished videos and dance music, unafraid to be openly gay. This trend for funk-pop is a powerful one: the music continues to play on sex appeal and elevates a black artist to the central role, but if we look a little closer we can see that the *favela* has become a backdrop, it has been normalised, from the margins to the cultural mainstream.

FEMINIST FUNK PLAYLIST

Elza Soares
A Carne
2002

MC Carol
Não Foi Cabral
2016

MC Rebecca
Cai de Boca
2018

Ludmilla e Anitta
Favela Chegou
2019

Elza Soares
Malandro
2007

Karol Conka
Lalá
2017

Jojo Todynho
Que Tiro Foi Esse
2017

MC Carol e Karol Conka
100% Feminista
2016

Deize Tigrona
Injeção
2014 (remix)

Anitta
Vai Malandra
2017

Ludmilla
Fala Mal de Mim
2014

Tati Quebra Barraco
Sou Feia Mas Tô na Moda
2004

MALANDRO AND MALANDRAGEM

When the Brazilian singer Anitta chose the title 'Vai Malandra' for one of her songs, she was using a key word in Brazilian popular culture, one with a long history that most Brazilians will understand. *Malandragem* is the culture of the *malandro*; a *malandro* is sharp witted, a conman, a petty criminal, a bar hustler, and as samba was seen as suspect music from the slums, *sambistas* were the quintessential *malandros*. In his 1935 novel *Jubiabá*, Jorge Amado gives a fascinating wider definition of the word: he uses it as a synonym for freedom. So the *malandro* is essentially a free man – free from the bonds of shared morality, personal ethics and social principles. In her 1994 song 'Malandragem', the great singer Cássia Eller sung a beautiful verse: 'I ask God / for just a little *malandragem* / because I am a boy / and I don't know the truth. I'm a poet and I haven't learned to love.' If we had to think of an environment that embodies the ethos of *malandragem* better than any other, we should look to the carnival. Carnival is the triumph of *malandragem*, the break from normality in which anything goes – although, particularly in the past, this applied only to men. When Anitta used the word in the feminine, *malandra*, she was subverting the rules and transferring this status of freedom to women, a seemingly small thing that is, in fact, a very big deal.

The queen of this trend is Rio-born Larissa de Macedo Machado, aka Anitta. With an astronomical number of followers on social media, she has broken into the crucial music industry circuit of TV, festivals, radio and awards. Anitta sings well but makes no claims to be the next Elis Regina; she is beautiful, but in her now famous video for 'Vai Malandra' she sent out a message to hundreds of millions of Brazilian women (based on the number of views) that they shouldn't be ashamed of their cellulite. The video, shot on the rooftops of a *favela* that, while real, resembles a Broadway set, showcases the fashion that jettisons bikinis for duct tape. Metres and metres of tape stuck to the body, creating perfectly defined tan lines and covering the barest minimum. Power also lies in defects and imperfections. As strange as it may seem, Anitta's proclamation is inspirational. Wearing duct tape, showing your cellulite and *brincando com o bum-bum* (shaking your booty) can also become acts of resistance. The *malandro* is losing ground because Anitta has become the *malandra*.

It is no coincidence that these new stars of the brand of funk that identifies as pop or rap almost always choose the *favela* as the setting for their videos, because the *favela* is the archetypal place where black Brazilian women have lived and continue to live in subjugation (even though it is by no means the only place where this happens). In the video for 'Cabeça de Nego' ('Black Mind'), a melodic rap in which the words this time count more for their sound, for what they evoke, we see Karol Conka – born Karoline dos Santos in 1987 to a poor family near Curitiba in the south of the country – striding through the *favela* of Boqueirão in São Paolo's South Zone. What is important is the figure of a woman like Karol carving out her own

> 'The era of the most radical right-wing government since the end of the dictatorship is also the era of the toughest female resistance.'

space for freedom in that context. In another of her famous videos, 'Vogue do Gueto' ('Ghetto Vogue'), Karol asks the listener 'Where can your glance take you? Could it be that our mental blindness has got us stuck in time? Our echo can break the system.'

DARK TIMES

On 7 August 2019 commemorative events took place across Brazil to mark the thirteenth anniversary of Maria da Penha's Law. That day the minister of justice at the time, Sérgio Moro, tweeted that men use violence against women because they feel under pressure and don't accept women's progress. His remarks may have been made in good faith but still drew on the same old cliché that men feel threatened. The minister emphasised that this violence happens because, in spite of what we might think, women are no longer the weaker sex, they are 'stronger and there are more of them than us and we have to recognise that they are better'. Moro, the former judge in the famous Lava Jato investigation (see 'Operation Car Wash' on page 19), was, until 2020, the strongman of the far-right government led by Jair Bolsonaro, the former army captain who was elected president after a largely unremarkable political career distinguished by his homophobic, misogynistic and racist views. As he got closer to the presidency, the rise of Bolsonaro certainly contributed to the reawakening of the country's feminist consciousness, which achieved some of its highest levels of visibility during the 2018 election campaign. It was expressed through the #EleNão (#NotHim)

movement (see page 49), which emerged on social media to counter the aggressive outbursts from Bolsonaro, who is a symbol of the white male-chauvinist power that discriminates against civil rights and minorities of all kinds. Many musicians joined in. Even though it attracted plenty of attention, the movement didn't manage to affect the outcome of the election, but its very existence was a new development in the history of ideologies in Brazil, so it is no coincidence that the feminism embraced by black artists is now stronger than was previously imaginable.

The era of the most radical right-wing government since the end of the dictatorship is also the era of the toughest female resistance. And it is significant that a book by the black feminist sociologist Djamila Ribeiro should have hit the bestseller list at precisely this moment. The question asked by the author in her title is *Quem Tem Medo do Feminismo Negro?* ('Who's Afraid of Black Feminism?'), which is not so surprising given that the murder of Marielle Franco was not just the first political assassination since the end of the dictatorship but was above all a sexist murder, the crime of a man who hated a woman and hated her in particular because she was a black bisexual activist from the *favela*. What her murderers were unable to kill off was the echo that Karol Conka spoke of in her song: an echo that can break the system. ✒

The baile funk movement has been criticised for its violent, vulgar lyrics that denigrate women. In the songs women are depicted as sex objects and are often referred to as *cachorras* (dogs) or *popozudas* (big butts), and there is frequent talk of desire for *novinhas* (youngsters).
Above: A woman dances on stage at a baile funk event displaying her legs and genitals to the crowd.
Below: A woman dancing at an event at Nitro Night, a club in São Paulo.

Above: A dancing couple simulate sexual intercourse.
Below: A group of men at a baile funk event in São Paulo force a woman to remove her underwear before photographing and filming her.
The photographs on these pages reveal the male-chauvinist reality of most of these venues.

Prime Time

For decades Rede Globo's programming has determined Brazilians' evening routine: the news, followed by a *telenovela* and a football match. The media group is hugely powerful, and while its direct influence on politics has waned since the days when its founder Roberto Marinho decided whether a government would stand or fall, it still holds considerable sway in the country thanks to its *telenovelas*.

ALEX CUADROS

Left and pages 62 and 75: Scenes from *Bom Sucesso*, a *telenovela* produced and broadcast by Rede Globo, premiered in July 2019, replacing *Verão 90*. It stars Grazi Massafera, Rômulo Estrela, David Junior, Antônio Fagundes, Ingrid Guimarães, Fabiula Nascimento, Armando Babaioff and Sheron Menezzes.

*'We would like to have the power to fix everything
that doesn't work in Brazil.'*

— Roberto Marinho

There's an image I often remember from a trip to Altamira, in the Amazon state of Pará. At one point I visited the *baixões*, or lowlands, a district of faded wooden shacks on stilts in a floodplain by the highway leading into town. Kids ran around in dirty clothes on uneven walkways spanning trash-strewn, murky water. It was the worst poverty I'd ever seen in Brazil, but, up on the sagging roofs above, I noticed pristine satellite dishes. As far as they were from the centres of wealth, the people there were connected through television to some version of Brazil's shared story. I'd been missing out on this story by failing to keep a TV in my apartment.

I realised my mistake hanging out in my ninth-floor living room one night, when from outside I heard shouts of 'Chupa, Carminha!' Living in São Paulo I was used to hearing my neighbours shout insults at one another. It happened whenever two São Paulo football teams faced off. After a goal, first would come the incredulous shrieks resolving into joy or despair in stereo around me, then fireworks: that rapid-fire crack-crack-crack-crack-crack, pause – then a deep boom – and then a fan in a football shirt would lean out from his balcony and yell 'Chupa, Palmeiras!' – 'Suck it, Palmeiras!' Later I knew the scores were level when another fan shouted 'Chupa, Corinthians!' This was different. Carminha turned out to be a character in a *telenovela* called *Avenida Brasil*, and that night was the finale. A shrieking conniver, she'd just taken a slap to the face. In a country of two hundred million people, eighty million were tuned in. *Novela* finales often drew huge audiences, but this was the biggest in years. The only other time Brazilians dropped everything else to plant themselves in front of the TV like this was when the national team played in the World Cup, and the divisions between Palmeiras and Corinthians disappeared.

I didn't get *telenovelas*. I'd seen *Avenida Brasil* on at the gym, but whatever was

ALEX CUADROS is an American journalist and author who spent six years in Brazil as a reporter for *Bloomberg* and other news outlets. He has written for *The New Yorker*, *The Atlantic*, *The Washington Post*, *Slate* and The Awl website reporting from Iraq, Colombia, Mexico and Venezuela as well as Brazil. His work has been supported by the Alicia Patterson Foundation and the Pulitzer Center. This article is an extract from his first book, *Brazillionaires* (Spiegel & Grau USA/Profile Books UK, 2016), which was nominated for the Financial Times and McKinsey Business Book of the Year Award and was also one of the books of the year in *The New York Times*.

special about it was lost on me. When I asked a Brazilian colleague in the Bloomberg newsroom what was so good about it, he said it was just good. As far as I could tell, it had little to do with the actual plot. Like all *novelas*, this one was written as it aired, adapting to the hopes and complaints of viewers six nights a week, and the twists were as endless and hard to swallow as always. Media critics latched on to two reasons for *Avenida Brasil*'s success. One was that it set a new standard for production values, with smoky cinematic shots of, say, the garbage heap on which one of the characters was abandoned as a little girl. The other was that its characters hailed to an unprecedented degree from the emerging middle class. Until recently *novelas* had mostly stuck to a thin slice of Ipanema privilege where chesty, perfectly bestubbled men in crisp white blazers break the hearts of gorgeous blonde ladies in palatial homes, complete with fireplaces, however impractical in balmy Rio. Previously poor Brazilians now had money to buy stuff: washing machines, smartphones, plane tickets, cars. What with the growing economy and social policies of the Workers' Party years, half the population now fitted into what Brazilian economists called classe C, with household incomes that went from a few hundred to a few thousand dollars a month. Advertisers were willing to pay to reach them. And, like anyone, these new consumers wanted to see people like themselves on screen.

People translate the word *telenovela* as soap opera, but that understates its place in the culture. In a country where cinema arrived late, *novelas* were wildly popular as a staple of radio long before the *tele* was tacked on. On TV they play during prime time, and everyone watches them, men and women alike. Even on an average

night *Avenida Brasil* drew three-quarters of the national viewership. 'If I can make something that is watched every night by seventy million people,' the director of *Avenida Brasil* said, 'why in the world would I want to go to Hollywood?' In the seven months that it ran, *Avenida Brasil* reportedly raked in a billion dollars in ad revenue. It may be the highest-grossing *novela* in Brazil's history.

But Rede Globo, the network that produced it, is used to dominating the market like this. Globo's programming was at the centre of an old Brazilian routine: you watch the nightly news on *Jornal Nacional*, you watch Globo's nine o'clock *novela* and, if there's a football match on that night, it starts when the *novela* is over. In recent years the network has lost ground to the internet and cable TV, but more than half of all money spent on TV ads in Brazil still goes to Globo. By 2012, when I started looking into its finances, the group brought in $6 billion a year in revenues. Today the sons of Globo's founder, Roberto Marinho, run the conglomerate, which encompasses TV, newspapers, magazines and radio stations. Outside politics, no other family has wielded as much influence in Brazil's national affairs. A former president, Fernando Henrique Cardoso, once referred to Globo as an 'institution of power' in Brazil. It's shaped the debate on wealth, sex and race for the past half-century.

Roberto Marinho is a bogeyman of the left, and with good reason. Marinho helped bring the military regime to power, running outright propaganda on Radio Globo and inflammatory editorials in his newspaper to drum up support for the coup in 1964. His most infamous distortion came in 1984, in the twilight of the regime, when hundreds of thousands of protesters took to the streets of São Paulo to demand free elections and a TV Globo anchor surreally claimed they were out there celebrating the city's birthday.

To much of the business class, Marinho is a symbol of entrepreneurship. Even though he was born into the media biz, he made the most of it. His father, a Rio de Janeiro newspaper tycoon, founded *O Globo* in 1925 but died of a heart attack three weeks later. Roberto was left in control at just twenty-one years old. He'd already worked as his father's secretary, but he wisely took the back seat at first. He watched and learned how to do the news before taking over as publisher six years later. Eventually his younger brothers joined the business, but Roberto was the one with the instinct for expansion. Over the next couple of decades he started a radio network and additional newspapers to serve different niches. As in many other parts of the world, the press in Brazil back then was openly partisan – sometimes sponsored outright by political parties – and willing to bury bad news about companies that paid for ads. Roberto Marinho was early in championing the 20th-century American press ideals of objectivity and neutrality. He liked to quote Arthur Miller's contention that a good newspaper is a nation talking to itself. He imagined he spoke not for himself but for Brazilians in general, channelling what he called 'public opinion' – except Marinho's idea of public opinion reflected his own convictions: anti-communist, pro-business, pro-democracy but also sympathetic to the military.

Marinho arrived late to the TV game. By the time Globo started airing in 1965 the leading network, TV Tupi, had been in operation for fifteen years. A few things set Globo apart. One was a loophole Marinho found in the constitution, which banned foreigners from investing in local broadcasters. Since it was vague

on profit-sharing arrangements, he struck a deal with the American firm Time, Inc. to inject several million dollars into his enterprise. This allowed him to buy the best equipment and hire the best talent. Another thing was Marinho's management style, which had no apparent logic but worked just the same. Despite the money from Time, TV Globo started as a shoestring operation, and yet Marinho hardly read financial statements, focusing instead on the big picture. He was reserved but authoritarian; his brother Rogério once said, 'When he lowered his voice, it was terrible.' He expected people to trust his intuitions, often without any explanation other than, 'You see the world as an ocean, noticing only the bubbles. What's going on down below, only I know.' After a year on air, discouraged by the network's slow take-off, Marinho's brothers sold their shares to him. Time got out in 1969, frustrated by the lack of profits. Still, Marinho was so sure about Globo's future that when he bought out his American partner he put up his own house as collateral for a loan. The network didn't turn a profit till 1971.

Probably the most important ingredient to Marinho's success was his gift for delegating responsibility, despite his love of control. In the mid-sixties he brought on two brilliant execs from Brazil's fledgling TV industry, Walter Clark and a man everyone knows as Boni, and offered them a share in the earnings. With their shirts unbuttoned to show off their chest hair and large pointy collars askew, they clashed with the suit-and-tie style Marinho favoured. They were three decades his junior, but he trusted them with rich budgets, and, with their instincts for smart programming, they played a key role in making Globo profitable. One important break came in 1966, when torrential

The first Brazilian politician whose (mis)fortunes were linked to Globo was Getúlio Vargas, who was swept to power in 1930 by a coup d'état carried out by a faction of the army also supported by Roberto Marinho. Getúlio is a legendary figure, on the one hand a pitiless dictator who idealised Mussolini and tortured communists, on the other the venerated 'father of the poor', as he was known in his propaganda but also by millions of Brazilians. Getúlio brought in the minimum wage, paid holidays, social security and trade unions, while steering the country into industrialisation. 'He took an entire nation from a state of semi-slavery and transformed us into citizens with rights,' Lula said of him. His Estado Novo, inspired by Mussolini in Italy and Salazar in Portugal but also by Roosevelt's New Deal, lasted until the end of the Second World War, when Getúlio was forced to resign, having made enemies of the army, the newspapers – including O Globo – and the middle classes. He was re-elected president in free elections in 1951 but was told to resign again by the army three years later. This time, instead of complying, Getúlio shot himself in the heart, causing an emotional outpouring in the country, with hundreds of thousands of people in mourning filling the streets of Rio. In the letter he left behind, the contents of which was broadcast on the radio, he accused international and local groups of having waged an 'underground campaign' against his administration. 'I have nothing left to give you but my blood ... I have given you my life. Now I offer you my death. Without fear. I am serenely taking my first step on the road to eternity and leaving my life to enter history.'

rains hit Rio and Clark cancelled the whole TV schedule for wall-to-wall coverage of what turned out to be some of the worst flooding in the city's history. The public was riveted. Anchors announced an initiative called SOS Globo, asking viewers to send in clothes and food for flood victims, and this also won points for the network. Almost overnight the little-known station earned a big reputation.

Rare for an entrepreneur, Marinho was already past sixty when he started TV Globo, the business that would define him. At times he could seem immortal. Even in his eighties he would joke about Globo's future, saying, 'if I'm no longer around one day ...' rather than when. He kept working till dementia hit in his final years.

Roberto Marinho believed in the revolution of 1964, as he called it, and the regime did repay his support by buying lots of ads, an old government tradition. Brazil became a TV nation watching Globo. By the seventies destitute families might not have had running water, but they usually had a TV set, like the poor families in today's baixões. Joe Wallach, an American exec Marinho hired away from Time Inc., explained what this meant. 'For the first time – it was incredible – a kid in Copacabana saw the buffalo off in the Amazon, and he didn't know that existed in the country. And over in Belém too, the Indians could see the buildings of Rio de Janeiro.' This was a big deal in a country where, for much of its history, the major cities had kept more contact with Portugal than with one another.

It was in the eighties that Marinho's monopoly reached its peak. Globo averaged ratings of 80 per cent, and, in a country where a quarter of the population still couldn't read, a fact was not truly a fact until it appeared on Jornal Nacional. As the military regime wobbled and prepared to

ÉRAMOS SEIS | globoplay

bow out, this gave Marinho the power to shape the political narrative that would be unusual in the history of any country. There's a saying, probably born in those years: 'In Brazil, television isn't a concession of the state, the state is a concession of television.'

Marinho's influence helps explain why the transition from the dictatorship back to democracy was more of a glide than a rupture. He helped to moderate the contesting interests – and he was proud of his role. To justify his cover-up of the free-election protests of 1984 he said he feared they could incite unrest and lead the military to crack down again. One of his sons remembers a military helicopter hovering outside TV Globo's windows one day, an implicit threat.

And yet Marinho turned against the status quo the following year after the free-election movement failed, as Congress was set to vote on the first civilian president in two decades. Snubbing Paulo Maluf, the candidate favoured by the generals, Marinho instead backed Tancredo Neves from the opposition. It was this that gave many regime-allied lawmakers the courage to defect. Most would agree that, by shooting down Maluf, Marinho did the people of Brazil a favour, but he also reaped lucrative favours for himself. Tancredo knew he stood no chance of putting the country back together without Globo's support, so he presented his cabinet picks one by one for Marinho's approval. To lead the communications ministry, which would oversee TV Globo, Marinho suggested a friend of his – Antonio Carlos Magalhães, known as ACM. Much to the displeasure of his party, the PMDB, Tancredo accepted. 'I'll fight with the pope, I'll fight with the Catholic Church, I'll fight with the PMDB, with anyone,' Tancredo explained, 'I just

won't fight with Dr Roberto.' Tancredo died before taking office, but José Sarney, the vice-president who took Tancredo's place, did Marinho the same courtesy.

While ACM was still minister, Marinho gave his family the contract to run a Globo affiliate in his home state of Bahia. After Sarney stepped down, the ex-president got the same deal in Maranhão. These contracts were not only highly profitable but a powerful platform to win votes for their ongoing political careers. Marinho also distributed these contracts to congressmen, giving him sway in the legislature. These partnerships may explain why, even though the new democratic constitution called for a ban on media monopolies and oligopolies – like Marinho's – Congress never drew up the legislation to implement it. Today these TV stations still serve as pillars of power for the regional bosses Brazilians call coronéis, or colonels.

Marinho was one of the three Brazilians on the first global Forbes list of billionaires, published in 1987. But he was much bigger than the other two, Sebastião Camargo and Antônio Ermírio de Moraes. In an interview with The New York Times that year Marinho acknowledged his status as a kind of unelected branch of government in the new democracy. 'I use this power,' he said, but, he added, 'I always do so patriotically, trying to correct things, looking for the best paths for the country. We would like to have the power to fix everything that doesn't work in Brazil. We dedicate all our power to this.' Walter Clark, the former Globo exec, compared Roberto Marinho to Citizen Kane's Charles Foster Kane, only without a Rosebud. But he wasn't as cold in his cunning as some believed. His responsibility weighed on him. He used to say that if he ever wrote his memoirs he would title them Condemned to Success. He suffered from anxiety and scraped at

'In Brazil, television isn't a concession of the state, the state is a concession of television.'

his own flesh with his fingernails, leaving blood on his papers. He took pills to get to sleep; once he overdosed and nearly died. And he was troubled by the times he chose the wrong path.

In 1989 Marinho threw his weight behind a politician who promised to modernise the nation but ended up making Brazil look like a banana republic. It was the first free presidential election in three decades, and the country was in turmoil. Lula was running and talked about breaking up Globo if elected, so Marinho understandably backed his opponent, a handsome young politician named Fernando Collor de Mello, who controlled a Globo affiliate in his home state of Alagoas. With Globo's help, he framed himself as a political outsider who would slim down a bloated state and sweep the corrupt 'maharajas' of Brasilia from power. On TV and in his newspapers Marinho gave a lot of space to Collor's warnings that Lula would bring 'disorder, fanaticism and insanity'. Globo also ran a *novela* that year titled *Que Rei Sou Eu?* ('What King Am I?'), in which all the politicians of a mystical Kingdom of Avilan are corrupt save for a young prince who takes power in the end. Collor actually referred to the *novela* once in a speech, saying that he was fighting against a real-life Kingdom of Avilan in Brazil.

Brazilian elections have two rounds, and Lula and Collor made it to the run-off. A few days before the vote, the race was neck and neck. For the final debate Marinho sent his top exec, Boni, to advise Collor. He probably didn't need to. After trouncing Collor in the previous debate, this time Lula appeared tired and sweaty. He spoke poorly, and most observers

agreed he'd lost. Still, when Marinho saw TV Globo's post-lunch recap the next day he said it made Lula look too good. And so on *Jornal Nacional* that night the producers cut together all Lula's worst moments and all Collor's best, and, as Boni himself would later phrase it, Collor's 3-2 victory became a 3-0. Official campaigning had come to an end by then, so Globo's was the last word on the race before the vote. It's hard to say how much that swung the result, but Collor won. Collor was a disaster. He led Brazil into the worst recession in its history even as salacious corruption scandals erupted inside the presidential palace.

Marinho eventually distanced himself from Collor, not that he had much to worry about. Even while protesting Globo's candidate, students sang a song from a Globo miniseries – *Anos Rebeldes* ('Rebel Years') – about youths who'd stood up to the dictatorship. Collor resigned, but Congress impeached him anyway. In typical Brazilian fashion, though, he was never convicted and everyone ended up friends. Elected a senator years later, he joined Lula's coalition in Congress. Lula never was the kind to hold a grudge. Ever the pragmatist, he also saw the value in making up with Globo. And so, when Dr Roberto died in 2003 at ninety-eight years old, Lula declared three days of official mourning. More to the point, he kept up the government ad budget, funnelling hundreds of millions of dollars to Globo each year, much as the military regime had done.

I got to meet one of the Globo heirs not long after the finale of *Avenida Brasil*, the billion-dollar *novela*. Marinho's three sons each own an equal slice of the empire and do their part to maintain it. The

THE PASSENGER Alex Cuadros

Above: A man watches
a *telenovela* in a café
in central São Paulo.

eldest takes care of the business side, the youngest heads up the Roberto Marinho Foundation and the middle son – João Roberto, who agreed to speak with me – runs the news operation. They've done well. Even though it has lost market share in recent years, Globo is more profitable than ever. Dr Roberto was worth a billion dollars when he died; nine years later, when we added up the family fortune at Bloomberg, we arrived at a total of $25 billion. Individually, each brother was almost as rich as Rupert Murdoch, the Australian-American media magnate who owns the Fox Corporation, *The Wall Street Journal* and *The Times* (London).

I went to see João Roberto with a Bloomberg editor from New York. We took a taxi to a narrow, non-descript building on a quiet street in Jardim Botânico, a wealthy neighbourhood in Rio. I saw none of the glamour I expected from a company with so many celebrities on its payroll. From a dingy lobby, a receptionist led us through a turnstile, down in an elevator, across an underground parking garage and

into a separate building where we passed through another set of turnstiles. We were handed off to another receptionist, and she led us up a dark stairwell, through a hallway and another set of doors. Here and there guards manned our roundabout route, which suggested complex security precautions, a power that needed hiding. We arrived at last at a door that swung open to reveal the billionaire heir we'd come to see. He extended his hand and introduced himself, as if it were necessary: 'João Marinho.' Wiry and tall, sixty years old but youthful looking, João wore thick-rimmed tortoiseshell glasses, a dark-blue blazer rumpled in the back, slacks of a subtly different dark blue, a white shirt and no tie. He was less formal than his dad had been. His office was spacious but not extravagant, except for the view through the floor-to-ceiling glass walls on two sides: lush green Rio hills, a shimmering Guanabara Bay, Sugarloaf Mountain. I guessed the glass was bulletproof.

The Bloomberg editor started the conversation tactfully with small talk. He remarked on the beauty of Rio, also on the terrible traffic. For a moment João looked mystified before politely nodding. I gathered he was a helicopter man. I knew the Marinhos had installed a helipad at their 1,300-square-metre (14,000 ft²) mansion near Paraty, down the coast from Rio. Built in the middle of an ecological reserve, in apparent breach of environmental laws, the home had won the Wallpaper Design Award for its sleek concrete-and-glass architecture. João spoke carefully, quietly, properly – in English, for the benefit of the editor. The family rarely talks to the press, perhaps since they own so much of it, but João said they admired Bloomberg. This gave me a funny sense of being a piece in some imaginary game of Risk among global billionaires. *Bloomberg Markets* magazine's 'World's Richest People' issue had just come out, so at one point I pulled a copy out of my bag and asked him what he thought of it. 'Yes, I've seen it,' João said. 'But we don't like to be on this list. We don't want to be known for that' – by which I understood money. 'We want to be known for what we do.'

When João talked about his family he conveyed a sense of time much broader than mine. He showed us a photo on the wall of his father at a desk in *O Globo*'s newsroom in the fifties and said he looked at it every day to remind himself where he came from. Although he'd inherited his fortune, João conveyed the idea that he'd earned it, too. He told us how he'd worked his way up as a Globo journalist before becoming news chief in the mid-nineties. It's a version of meritocracy that makes sense if João sees himself not merely as an

individual but as the standard-bearer of a long-term project, a lineage, a dynasty. The way João described it, he and his brothers are like stewards of Brazil. They seek to guide the nation as their father did. 'To have a presence like we do in society gives us a permanent sense of responsibility,' he said. Planning for the next generations of Globo shareholders, João and his brothers have already drawn up rules for their children and grandchildren. To join the family business, heirs have to get MBAs. Enter religion or politics, and they'll forfeit their shares' voting rights.

The Marinhos are trying to change Globo's image of bias. They need to now if they want to stay on top of an increasingly competitive market. In a section on Globo's website titled 'Errors' they now acknowledge two, their most famous ones: the cover-up of free-election protests in 1984 and the editing of Lula's debate with Collor in 1989. There's a much longer section on the website titled 'False Accusations'. Hoping to straighten the historical record, the brothers have distanced themselves from their dad's politics – sort of. When they repudiated *O Globo*'s support for the 1964 coup, a *Jornal Nacional* anchor read the editorial live. They lamented the regime's human-rights abuses, but they also praised its economic advances. It was a curious balancing act: a concession to public opinion on the one hand; a defence of their family's convictions on the other.

What are their convictions? João mentioned two: better education and small government, both old banners of Roberto Marinho. The first is hard to argue with. The second is complex. In the editorial

Roberto Marinho died of a stroke on 6 August 2003 at the age of ninety-eight. He was a vain man who had 5,328 ties in his wardrobe and who wore shoes with a discrete internal heel to raise him above his natural height of 163 centimetres. He had a passion for horses and was a successful steeplechaser, forcing the producers of *Jornal Nacional* to broadcast long clips of his victorious laps. He invited Globo photographers to document parties at his house in Rio, attended by artists and businessmen. His villa was hidden away at the foot of Mount Corcovado, modelled on an 18th-century sugar baron's estate. Marinho hired the landscape artist Roberto Burle Marx to design his gardens, and he filled the house with paintings and bought a six-by-six-metre tapestry by the celebrated French artist Jean Lurçat. A patron of the arts, Marinho was also a literary figure, occupying seat number thirty-nine at the Brazilian Academy of Letters. As well as being vain, he was also somewhat vindictive, as illustrated by an episode described in his official biography. At the start of the military regime he refused to support the political ambitions of a militant journalist named Carlos Lacerda, who had been named governor of Rio and had previously been his ally in the fight against Getúlio Vargas. Lacerda publicly attacked Marinho. In his biography Marinho revealed that one day he tucked a revolver into his belt and went to Lacerda's house to kill him. The guards recognised Marinho and let him in, but Lacerda had been informed ahead of time and had fled before his arrival.

pages of *O Globo*, the Marinhos will declare that a wealth tax like the one proposed by the French economist Thomas Piketty is simply unworkable, without hinting that they might have a stake in the issue. The family deplored how the state had grown under the Workers' Party, but they didn't mention any of the government's massive Globo ad buys. Possibly to protect this subsidy, João told me they restricted their opinions to the editorial pages of *O Globo* and kept the TV network, with all its power to influence the debate, non-partisan. The opinions seep through anyway. Sometimes it's a question of focus. Although cases of fraud are rare among the fifty million Brazilians who depend on Bolsa Família, the Workers' Party welfare programme, they're covered frequently on the Globo network. Meanwhile tax evasion estimated in the hundreds of billions of dollars a year gets relatively short shrift (perhaps because Globo itself is fighting charges that it evaded taxes). At other times complex national debates are resolved before they ever reach the viewer. To weigh in on Brazil's labour laws, producers will invite an orthodox economist to explain how they raise the cost of doing business but rarely a unionist to speak about the protections they provide.

As a journalist, obsessively reading the papers each day, I can forget that most people don't care too much about politics. Voting is obligatory here, but informing yourself is not, and in surveys just weeks after elections a third of Brazilians can't remember which congressman they voted for. As many as one in ten will show up at the polling station and vote for no one – you can do that. Partly this reflects the old fatalism here about politicians, all corrupt. Even apolitical Brazilians, though, watch *telenovelas*. This is where much of Globo's influence lies. João knew his family's

power to set the cultural agenda. He told me about Globo's tradition of inserting 'social messaging' in *novelas* to make a difference in society. This works. A Globo *novela* with poignant stories of romantic separation helped move Congress to approve the first legal framework for divorce in 1977. Since they run for just one season, *novelas* can be cultural milestones. *Avenida Brasil* was a milestone in part because it put the emerging middle class on screen in a big way.

Still, I noticed something off about Globo's portrait of classe C. Although the *novela* took place on Rio's heavily black north side, the top black role was that of a maid. This is an old tradition. From early on in Globo *novelas*, a black actress in her maid's outfit might dust off a candelabra as a blonde teared up about her husband's infidelity in the foreground. For most black actresses the best they could hope for was to play a maid who got involved in the story somehow. When Globo adapted *Uncle Tom's Cabin* into a *novela* in 1969 the producers cast a white actor as Uncle Tom. He wore blackface, with little corks in his nostrils to widen his nose and cotton balls in his mouth to slum down his Portuguese. The same actor also played Abraham Lincoln, who'd been written into the plot line. Blacks did get to play the slaves. In one *novela* a white actor says of a maid he's fallen in love with, 'What does it matter if she's coloured if her soul is white and pure?' In an interview once, a Globo *novela* director explained that putting blacks on TV was just bad for business, since the people who had money then, the people advertisers wanted to reach, were almost all white. Blacks started to get more space in Globo storylines in the eighties, but even now they play few leading roles. Watching Globo, you could be forgiven for thinking that the vast majority of Brazilians are white. This, even though slightly more than half of the population identifies as *pardo* (mixed race, literally brown) or *preto* (truly black).

It's hard to blame Roberto Marinho for all this. While he loved the news he left *novelas* in the hands of his deputies. He

'Roberto Marinho did seem to harbour unresolved racial anxieties: all his life he put rice powder on his face to disguise his dark complexion.'

did, though, seem to harbour unresolved racial anxieties: all his life he put rice powder on his face to disguise his dark complexion. In this way he was a creature of his country's traditions. Over more than three centuries Brazil imported nearly five million African slaves – ten times as many as the United States – and in 1888, when it became the last country in the Americas to abolish slavery, one major rationale was that it dirtied the racial mix. This idea played into a particularly Brazilian feeling of inferiority, which the author Nelson Rodrigues would later call *complexo de vira-lata*, mutt complex. Brazil's tiny elite believed the best way to catch up with the club of serious countries was by 'whitening' the population with immigrants from Europe. One reason a third of the people living in the state of São Paulo today have Italian blood is that the government paid ocean passage and set them up with jobs on coffee plantations. The hope was that they'd intermarry with people of African descent and produce lighter-skinned children. Race has always been fluid in Brazil, never binary like in the United States. Partly this was because of a history of miscegenation that stretched back to cosmopolitan Portugal; partly, since Portugal had so few inhabitants, racial mixing was a necessity in populating the colony. With so few native-born Brazilians of pure-white ancestry, some mixed-race people in Brazil managed to rise through the ranks of business and politics. Some ex-slaves even bought their own slaves. There's an old expression here, 'money whitens' – although the blacker you were

to begin with the harder it was to rise. And most didn't. As in most countries with a slave past, being born black in Brazil puts you at a disadvantage.

Even many socially progressive Brazilians cling to the idea that theirs is a post-racial paradise. Some activists blame the 'myth of racial democracy' for the fact that Brazil never had a black civil rights movement. A rapper from São Paulo, Emicida, has said, 'It's fucked up to have to fight a cordial kind of racism, one that doesn't show itself. You don't know who the enemy is because he never declares himself.' The sociologist Florestan Fernandes called it *preconceito de ter preconceito*, prejudice against being prejudiced. It's a fantasy of Brazil that glides over the fact that apartment buildings, mine included, still maintain 'service elevators' for maids who just happen to be overwhelmingly black, with 'social elevators' for everyone else. A black friend told me how, riding the social elevator in her building once, an old lady asked her suspiciously which apartment she worked in. Even today one in six women in Brazil's labour market works as a maid. During Dilma's presidency they would finally win rights as formal labourers: the minimum wage, overtime, a lunch break, social security, severance pay. The law caused a backlash among middle-class Brazilians who, because of low unemployment and higher wages, already found it increasingly difficult to afford a full-time servant. Some took to social media to voice their displeasure. With the anonymity of the internet, the cordiality peeled back. There's a Twitter

THE PASSENGER   Alex Cuadros

account, @AMinhaEmpregada (My Maid), that retweets comments about cleaning ladies. A typical find: 'The only black person whose complaining I can stand is my maid because she washes my underwear.'

Still, Brazilians would tell me that inequality here is a matter strictly of class, not race. It's true that there are whites in the *favelas*, too, but how many blacks do you ever see in the financial world? When I did interviews at banks, the only blacks I saw wore the hokey outfits of old-fashioned maids and butlers as they brought coffee to us on a silver tray. The divide starts early. The average poor white kid gets better schooling than the average poor black kid. Brazil's best universities are state run and cost nothing but are so competitive that, given the crappiness of basic public education, it's very hard to get in unless you can afford private school or private tutoring. When public universities adopted affirmative action starting in the early 2000s, many white Brazilians were outraged. TV Globo's news chief, Ali Kamel, wrote a book titled *Não Somos Racistas* ('We Are Not Racists') in which he complained that the quotas undermined the principle of meritocracy. It's a curious position for the employee of a company whose current owners were born into their places at the top of the pyramid.

A *novela* titled *Salve Jorge* had recently debuted when I met with João Marinho. It was the first to be shot largely on location in a *favela*. If it had a message it was to promote a new programme to install UPPs – Police Pacification Units – in Rio's one thousand *favelas*. João spoke enthusiastically about the programme, how it could transform the city. It was a big deal because *favelas* had become the semi-sovereign fiefdoms of drug gangs. The idea of the UPPs, hatched as Rio campaigned for the 2016 Olympics, was for police to sweep

THE CORDIAL MAN

The frequent use of the diminutive to describe things and people; the habit of addressing people by their first name rather than their surname in all circumstances; the desire for physical intimacy even in superficial relationships; the intimate relationship with religion. These are some of the characteristics of Brazilian 'cordiality' listed by Sérgio Buarque de Holanda in his book *Raízes do Brasil* (1936), which – at a crucial period in the country's history marked by the crisis of the old oligarchies as well as the expansion of the press and popular entertainment – helped to define Brazilian identity under the concept of the *homem cordial*, the cordial man. During the same period the anthropologist Gilberto Freyre developed a theory that 'harmony' between Brazil's different races was a historical necessity and 'miscegenation' its peaceful outcome. In reality, there was more subtlety to Buarque's argument: for him these characteristics arose from a way of being that did not reflect Brazilians' inner reality, leading people to place individualism over engagement with social issues. At the same time as reporting actual behaviour, Buarque was identifying a defect in society. Nevertheless, the concept of the cordial man proved popular and ultimately became a self-image – no matter how far removed from reality – alongside Freyre's supposed harmony. For the sociologist Jessé Souza, this helped to hide the skeleton on which the body of Brazilian society is supported, which perpetuates the violent, repressive, racist, 'slavocratic' model that, according to many observers, can explain the rise of a far-right leader like Jair Bolsonaro.

out the gangs with an overwhelming assault and then establish a permanent force that would, for the first time ever, build a relationship with the community. Public services would follow: sewers, garbage pickup, public transport, proper housing. The programme started with the *favelas* bordering nice, rich, touristy areas like Copacabana and Ipanema. Eventually it reached the location for *Salve Jorge*: Complexo do Alemão, an infamous stronghold for a gang known as the Comando Vermelho, or Red Command. It's in the city's working-class *subúrbio*, a long way north of the beach. Complexo do Alemão (the German's Compound) is so named because the land once belonged to a Pole. Close enough. Migrant families filled its hills starting in the fifties, and in the eighties the drug gangs took over. Usually the only state presence residents ever saw was when police stormed the alleyways hunting down *bandidos* in gun battles whose stray bullets ended plenty of innocent lives. Politicians cared about *favelas* only when elections came around. They would come and negotiate votes in return for the promise to build a day-care centre or a first-aid post. *Favelas* not under the control of drug traffickers might be ruled by cops who formed paramilitary gangs known as *milícias*.

The pacification of Alemão came in response to a wave of attacks across Rio in November 2010. Hoping to disrupt the Red Command's communication networks, the authorities had transferred imprisoned gang members to penitentiaries far from Rio, and the Red Command decided to show its power by coordinating high-profile hit-and-run robberies. At one point half a dozen armed men – apparently from Alemão – carried out an *arrastão*, blocking the Washington Luís Freeway to rob drivers. They set two cars on fire, and when a military vehicle happened on the scene they tossed a grenade at it. Brazil's drug gangs are alarmingly well armed. Over the next few days gang members ambushed police posts and set fire to city buses. The scale of the attacks frightened Brasília so much that the defence minister agreed to send in the military to take over Alemão. *Salve Jorge*'s first episode splices archival footage with dramatised scenes of the takeover. On the fourth and final day of the offensive, 2,700 men secured the perimeter in early-morning darkness. Sixty thousand people live in the complex of *favelas* that make up Alemão. As the invasion commenced, residents looked curiously from their windows. Others heaped furniture in front of their windows to shield against stray bullets. At 8 a.m. two military helicopters lifted into the sky. The government forces began their advance up narrow, steep roads overhung by clusters of DIY electric lines. Embedded with them, reporters and cameramen in flak jackets relayed it all live. Bulldozers pushed makeshift barricades out of the way, and, as the troops ascended the hill, taking cover behind armoured assault vehicles, *bandidos* took potshots from the back of a fleeing motorcycle or a notch in an unfinished cinderblock wall. The Red Command was well armed but poorly trained, and, despite their constant fire, they didn't cause a single casualty. They retreated, melting into the *favela*. By 10 a.m. the troops had reached the top of a hill where a cable-car station would soon go into operation. A soldier set off a green smoke flare to signal that official forces had secured the area. Everyone had expected bloodshed, but the mission was accomplished, just like that. The government had taken Alemão. Residents waved white flags from their windows, held up babies for the cameras. One group hoisted a banner that read *paz* – peace – with a backwards z. Up on the hill an army captain stabbed a flagpole into a patch of earth. The wind caught the flag, and the green and yellow and blue of Brazil flapped proudly in the wind. All that actually happened. In the *Salve Jorge* version

the captain thrusts his helmet into the air, whooping in triumph, smiling wide with his handsome strong jaw.

I paid a visit to Alemão to find out what its residents thought about Globo's take on their home. I got in touch with a local newspaper called *Voz da Comunidade* ('Voice of the Community'), and a 24-year-old journalist named Daiene Mendes volunteered to be my guide. We arranged to meet one evening at Bonsucesso train station, which connected to the cable car that would take us up into Alemão's hills. I felt a bit nervous visiting at night. Gang members who had lain low for a while after the pacification were now making noise again. There had been a shoot-out every day in recent weeks. Not long before my visit, the cable car had temporarily shut down because of stray bullets. But I didn't have long in Rio, and this was the time that Daiene could meet.

Daiene showed up in a puffy jacket against the mild Rio winter, and we took the cable car up with men and women returning from work in the city centre. Daiene was born and raised in Alemão. She told me about a youth in which school came second to playing *futebol* in the alleyways with her friends. That changed when she was fifteen, and her dad, a painter, heard about a class that paid students $40 a month. So she decided to attend. In the afternoons after school she trained to work as a monitor at one of Rio's museums, which meant greeting visitors and guiding them around. After working at a science museum not far from Alemão, she grew close to the administrators, and they recommended her for a museum job in the city centre – a long way from home. 'My horizons weren't just widened, they were stretched out,' she said. Before encountering the museum world she'd never read a book, but, when I met her, she was working towards a degree in journalism. Her exposure to a different Rio made her realise how much Alemão limited you. Most of her friends hadn't seen much outside the *favela* – except, she said, for what they watched on Globo.

On weekends, Daiene said, middle-class Brazilians now rode the cable car to observe *favela* life below. From the cables suspended above Alemão they could see the chaotic texture of a self-built town, kids piloting kites from rooftops here, girls in bikinis sunbathing on rooftops there, the reinforcing bars protruding from the concrete on all the rooftops, because homes were never quite finished in the *favela*; you could always add another level. The residents didn't necessarily see the tourists as gawkers or invaders. Mostly they were pleased that outsiders wanted to visit for once.

At the first station we got out and beheld the view. The sky was dark by now. With cheap white and yellow fluorescent bulbs making pricks of light in every direction, the complex of *favelas* resembled a night sky laid out carpet-like on to the contours of a craterous valley. 'It's prettier from here than up close,' Daiene said. As we walked down a freshly paved road leading from the cable car into the *favela*, I could see why the politically correct word for *favela* was *comunidade*. Everywhere we went – along narrow roads where little sedans barely squeezed past one another, through narrower pathways where old guys sat on steps shooting the shit, past the tight-tented stalls of a market where vendors sold fresh fruit or phone chargers, all of it thrumming with activity – everywhere we went, people shouted 'Oi, Daiene!' and she shouted 'Oi!' back. I felt safe with her.

After the government takeover, services really did arrive. The local utility firm came in and fixed up the power network. Lula's low-income housing programme funded new apartment complexes to replace old, sloping shacks. 'These were the first public works I had ever seen here,' Daiene told me, pointing out a housing project with bright, fresh-looking paint. Still, she said, the occupation didn't make all the problems go away. Other problems emerged. The soldiers occupying Alemão would kick down doors ostensibly looking for gang members, ransack people's homes and sometimes steal their valuables. In the *favela* some say the military dictatorship never ended. During informal interrogations by police, torture is commonplace. Summary executions are framed as 'resistance killings'. The victims are disproportionately black, young and male – although, in Rio at least, the cops are often young black men, too. Daiene, who's black herself, put it like this: 'It's poor black *favelados* killing poor black *favelados*, as usual.' The pacification programme was supposed to turn a relationship of violence into one of trust. That's a tricky task. The police clamped down on baile funk parties financed by drug gangs where kids dance to beats inherited from Miami bass, melodies sampled from everywhere and homespun raps. Working families appreciated their newly peaceful Saturday nights, but to many residents it felt like an imposition from above.

Favelados have a complex relationship with the gangs. When the state is absent they can act like an informal government, subsidising food for needy neighbours, charging for access to pilfered electricity and cable TV, preventing petty crime and dispensing primitive justice. Daiene said, 'I've been stopped by the police, but I never had any problems with the *tráfico* [the drug gangs]. They saw me grow up. They know my whole family. The police don't.'

The government had sold a utopia, Daiene said – something like Order and Progress. After soldiers planted the flag at the top of the hill the national anthem blared from a sound truck. 'Lots of people cried from the emotion of it all,' she said. 'I cried.' As far as she could see, though, the government had failed to deliver its utopia. Money meant to integrate *favelas* with the rest of the city dried up while projects for the 2016 Olympics ploughed ahead. Ipanema and Copacabana got a fancy bike-share system even as pacification police found themselves overextended, backsliding into their old role fighting *bandidos*.

Daiene introduced me to the owner of a clothing shop that sold T-shirts reading 'Favela: faço parte dela', 'Favela: I'm a part of it'. Sales had surged after the UPPs came, as kids with money from the beachy south side felt safe enough to visit for the first time ever. But now the violence had scared them off again. Some residents preferred the old days with the Red Command in control. The drug trade brought in money that recirculated at bars and restaurants and shops in the *favela*. This fatalism frustrated Daiene. I asked Daiene why she thought Globo wanted to film a *novela* at Alemão. 'There's this *favela* aesthetic,' she said. It's not just the cable car, foreign tourists now go on *favela* tours. She also knew that, for the first time since *favelas* began cropping up more than a century ago as Northeastern migrants flocked south to big cities, they were valuable to the national economy as more than a source of cheap labour. Eleven million Brazilians live in *favelas*, and their homes now have flat-screen TVs and laptops hooked up to Facebook – ordinary trappings of modern life that are nonetheless something new here.

Daiene introduced me to the founder of *Voz de Comunidade*, Rene Silva. He'd gained

Avenida Brasil was just the latest in a long line of smash hits that have had millions of Brazilians glued to their TV screens at 9 p.m. after the *Jornal Nacional* pursuing the notion that they were taking part in some great collective narrative. Some shows have been benchmarks in the history of television, ushering in a new era either through the size of their audiences or the issues covered and the actors they introduced. The big stars in Brazil come from TV shows rather than the cinema. Take *Vale Tudo* (1988), perhaps one of the biggest of all, which launched the careers of Glória Pires, Regina Duarte and Antônio Fagundes. The dictatorship had officially been over for three years; it was the year of the new constitutional charter. The story, written by two masters of the art, Gilberto Braga and Aguinaldo Silva, propelled previously undiscussed topics into the limelight and therefore into conversations on the street, at the hairdressers and on apartment-block landings: the scourge of corruption, the first covertly homosexual characters (who would be supressed or revived by the writers depending on the public mood) and finally a crime worthy of a film noir, the big question that became a genuine national obsession: who killed Odete Roitman? The character was played by a star with a big future ahead of her, Beatriz Segall. Other shows also marked the history of the genre: *Renascer* with its cocoa-plantation saga (1993); *O Rei do Gado* (1997); *Rainha da Sucata* (1990), the portrait of São Paolo's nouveaux riches; *Paraíso Tropical* (2007), in which the central character was a prostitute played by Camila Pitanga; and *Viver a Vida* (2009), where Taís Araújo became the first black actress to lead the cast of a prime-time *telenovela*.

some fame live-tweeting the military take-over, publishing first-hand information that even the embedded journalists couldn't get. Globo made him into a character in *Salve Jorge*. The head writer would sometimes call him up for advice. Globo never paid him for this, but it got his name out. He was one of those people born with an entrepreneurial instinct. He'd founded the paper when he was eleven, and, while it never made any money, it kept him afloat. Roberto Marinho probably had this instinct, but I wondered whether if his sons had been born in Alemão they would have clawed out their own little media business as Rene Silva has. I met Rene at the *Voz*'s offices, a cramped apartment where Daiene used to live, now filled with teenagers engrossed in vaguely productive chaos. Rene had an unruly Afro that he vanished into a beanie before standing up to chat with me. I asked him what he thought of *Salve Jorge*. He thought it was shallow. Apart from the occasional shoot-out for dramatic tension, all the social issues got smoothed over – like police abuse. The police in the *novela* were all heroes. He talked about the *favela*'s resistance to state authority, its nostalgia for gangsters, and wished Globo had explored these contradictions. 'It's a huge missed opportunity to help people understand why things are the way they are here,' he said. 'The *novela* was like, "People are poor but they're happy."'

And yet they do seem happy, despite everything. In one survey, 94 per cent of *favelados* said they considered themselves happy. They embody a very Brazilian contradiction: pessimistic about the system that surrounds them, optimistic about their own lives. Perhaps strangest of all, most people from Alemão didn't mind being packaged and pandered to. They loved *Salve Jorge*. They loved seeing so-and-so's bakery where they bought their loaves of bread. So what if the black characters on the show were just sidekicks to lighter-skinned protagonists? Everyone watched. And this pride emerged. In the past you'd be embarrassed to say you were from Alemão. The name conjured some kind of post-apocalyptic zone, so you'd say you were from a neighbouring area. That had changed now, not because of the UPPs but because of Globo. People started announcing it: I'm from Alemão – you know, like the *novela*.

These days Globo remains the most powerful force in TV – but much diminished by the rise of social media. In the 2018 presidential election the conglomerate's preferred candidate, a centre-right establishment figure, achieved less than 5 per cent of the vote. Instead, propelled by conspiracy theories and culture-war screeds that spread virally on Facebook and WhatsApp, the far-right former army captain Jair Bolsonaro proved victorious. Despite being a military man, Bolsonaro was in many ways anathema to the Globo heirs' cosmopolitan values – socially liberal, pro-free-market. Bolsonaro was openly anti-gay, and he had long espoused big-government ideas (although he ultimately appointed a University of Chicago-trained economy minister). Globo might be the left's old mortal enemy, but, as the network made its opposition to Bolsonaro clear, something strange happened: the president labelled the network a leftist tool. ✒

This article is an adapted and updated excerpt from the book *Brazillionaires*, published in 2016 by Spiegel & Grau in the USA and Profile Books in the UK.

Prosperity Now: The Rise of the Evangelicals

Brazil is seeing a boom in conversions to the neo-Pentecostal movement and in particular to the Universal Church of the Kingdom of God, which preaches prosperity theology: pay up and have faith. The bishop who leads the church is one of the country's richest men and the owner of Brazil's third-largest television network.

ANNA VIRGINIA BALLOUSSIER
Translated by Laura Garmeson

Left: A member of a neo-Pentecostal evangelical church meets a group of homeless people on the streets of São Paulo.

'Ugly, horrible, disgraceful thing,' the evangelical bishop Sérgio Von Helder exclaimed. Swathed in a grey jacket that looked a couple of sizes too big for him, he then aimed a series of kicks at the statue next to him: it was an icon of Our Lady of Aparecida, the most popular representation of the Virgin Mary in Brazil. The slicked-back hair, the poor production, the blue background, everything about the broadcast smacked of trashy live TV from the 1990s. The programme was aired by one of Brazil's largest television networks, Record, which just so happened to have been acquired six years before by the church to which the bishop was affiliated, a man whose fancy footwork could give Cristiano Ronaldo a run for his money.

Context: in the evangelical worldview the worship of idols and saints goes against God's will. This scene dominated the news cycle of a Brazil that was still predominantly Roman Catholic and provoked a violent reaction from a section of the population, resulting in attacks on churches of the denomination in question. The 'kicking of the saint', as the incident came to be known, tarnished the image of the Igreja Universal do Reino de Deus, the Universal Church of the Kingdom of God, but it didn't destroy it, as its enemies had predicted at the time.

Its leader, Bishop Edir Macedo, managed to bounce back, to the extent that in 2014 he even inducted into his religious empire some of the top-ranking officials from the same country that had, to use his own words, humiliated him years earlier. Today fortune seems to be in the evangelicals' favour, and the most famous face among their leaders is Macedo, a media magnate who occasionally makes an appearance like a vision of some white-bearded biblical prophet.

Brazil's last official population census revealed that between 2000 and 2010 the proportion of Catholics in the country fell from 74 to 64.6 per cent while the evangelicals grew from 15 to 22.2 per cent, a jump from 26 million to more than 42 million people. Today, a decade on, the Datafolha research institute estimates that evangelicals make up 32 per cent, while followers of the Vatican have fallen to half the Brazilian population – which, however, remains the largest concentration of Catholics in the world – and this downward trend is now in free fall.

When Macedo started preaching, nine out of ten Brazilians identified as Catholic. His Universal Church led the country's great neo-Pentecostal wave, a new branch of evangelicalism that brought with it two little magic words: prosperity theology. They claimed it was possible to bring down to the terrestrial plane, and not just confine to a distant afterlife, the promised pyrotechnics at the end of the tunnel. No more talk of having to suffer in this life to accumulate credit in the next. Now the rewards were instant: anyone who behaved like a good child of God would receive their blessings straight away, in this life. All you had to do was have faith – and, naturally, give money to the church.

Reginaldo Prandi, a professor of sociology at the University of São Paulo who specialises in Afro-Brazilian religions, discussed the phenomenon in an article in the *Folha de S. Paulo* newspaper: 'the

ANNA VIRGINIA BALLOUSSIER graduated in journalism from the Federal University of Rio de Janeiro. She is a Brazilian journalist who writes on religion for the *Folha de S. Paulo*, the country's leading newspaper.

'The neo-Pentecosals claimed it was possible to bring down to the terrestrial plane, and not just confine to a distant afterlife, the promised pyrotechnics at the end of the tunnel.'

Brazilian economy, which used to be weighted towards the worker who produces, is shifting towards the consumer', so the evangelicals have had to adapt. 'This new theology claims you can count on God to make all your consumerist dreams come true,' says the author of *A Realidade Social das Religiões no Brasil* ('The Social Reality of Religions in Brazil'). 'Essentially, it is no longer possible to identify a Pentecostal in a crowd by their clothes, hair or posture, as used to be the case. Everything has adjusted to the new living conditions in a country whose government boasts of the (dubious) emergence of a "new middle class" but who are, in fact, regular customers at the local cheap-goods store.'

While the Catholics were like an ocean liner, stuck on their course by the rigid hierarchy of the Holy See and still tied to traditions that had barely tolerated mass in the vernacular until the 1960s, the evangelicals were adapting like a jet-ski to the new religious tides. The Universal Church is the perfect example. Its brand of conservatism comes with a modern packaging. Take, for example, Godllywood, the project created by the women of the Universal Church, which was 'born out of anger at the immoral values our society has acquired from Hollywood'. Young people wearing black-and-green uniforms march and salute, declaring themselves 'ready for battle'; these are the 'Gladiators of the Altar' from Macedo's congregation, preparing to form battalions of new pastors across Brazil and in the ninety-two countries where the church claims to be active.

This new wave of evangelicalism has dominated late-night network TV and, nowadays, social media. With new churches opening on every corner, it has inspired puns like *templo é dinheiro* (the temple is money, a play on the Portuguese for time is money, *tempo é dinheiro*). In an interview with *Veja* magazine in 1997, one pastor, José Wellington Bezerra da Costa, head of the Assembly of God Bethlehem Ministry, the largest Pentecostal denomination in the country, joked, 'Wherever there is Coca-Cola, a post office and a branch of Bradesco bank, there's an Assembly of God.'

In 2013, while researching a report for the newspaper I work for, I attended the 2 o'clock service (there are several throughout the day) at a small Universal Church in central São Paulo. Members of the fifty-strong congregation were each given a piece of bread cut into pieces the size of a thumbprint and grape juice from a carton served in small white plastic cups like those used to serve coffee in an office, distributed by the *obreiros*, or labourers, as the pastor's assistants are called. Halfway through the nearly two-hour service the preacher, who was wearing a shiny red tie, made us all walk underneath a giant structure – made out of what appeared to be polystyrene and looked like it had been coloured with brown marker pen – which resembled an allegorical carnival float and was referred to as the Sinner's Archway.

To the outsider the church's services can seem somewhat theatrical. Many of them focus on issues that tend to be problematic for everyone and could easily fall

under the heading 'life coaching'. So, for example, at the imposing headquarters of the Universal Church, Mondays are dedicated to 'financial success', Tuesdays are for 'restoring physical and emotional health', on Wednesdays it's the turn of 'spiritual fortification' and the popular Friday slot promises to cure heartache with 'love therapy'. The week is rounded off with the 'prayer to eliminate stress and emotional burdens'.

This all takes place inside Edir Macedo's most ambitious project, the Temple of Solomon, an oversize replica of the biblical monument, which cost the Brazilian bishop nearly $300 million and symbolises the rise of the evangelicals in this country. Inside this edifice – constructed in stone imported from Israel – Macedo has received several presidents, from Dilma Rousseff of the Brazilian Workers' Party to Jair Bolsonaro.

Today, six years on from its inauguration, it is not unusual for the various daily services to be full. The space seats ten thousand people. The dress code prohibits the wearing of hats, sleeveless tops, football shirts, flip-flops, shorts, low-cut tops, miniskirts and sunglasses. This is all set out in the code of conduct published by the church for those who want to get to know the Temple of Solomon, 'the place where God has chosen to reside'. 'If you were going to meet God himself at his house, what would you wear?' asks Bishop Renato Cardoso, Edir Macedo's son-in-law, in a video released during their first year. 'Dress as though you were going to a social event to meet a very important person.'

'The Universal Church has revolutionised the religious landscape in Brazil,' says Christina Vital da Cunha, professor of sociology at Fluminense Federal University in Rio de Janeiro. 'Since its emergence there have been many changes

Left and above: The garden of the Temple of Solomon in São Paulo. The temple is a replica – albeit much larger – of the structure that once stood in Jerusalem. Inaugurated in 2014, it was built by the Universal Church of the Kingdom of God. Tourists can take a guided tour of the Bible-themed grounds adjoining the church.

'Over three decades the Universal Church's top-ranking members had amassed twenty-three television channels and forty radio stations as well as nineteen other companies.'

to the evangelical way of life. It was the first national evangelical denomination to have its own free-to-air TV channel. It has these grandiose churches, and its newspaper, *Folha Universal*, has an impressive weekly circulation: 2.5 million copies. The Brazilian Republican Party is a political party whose president is a bishop at the Universal Church, Federal Deputy Marcos Pereira.'

In the last Brazilian population census, in 2010, nearly two million Brazilians claimed to be followers of the Universal Church. But it is worth remembering that Edir Macedo, as well as being a spiritual leader, is also a seasoned media magnate. In addition to Record, his production company of the same name has in recent years released the two all-time biggest blockbusters in Brazilian cinema: *Nada a Perder* ('Nothing to Lose'), the first instalment of Macedo's biopic trilogy, and *Dez Mandamentos* ('The Ten Commandments'), a remake of the biblical story. The two films drew audiences of almost twelve million, surpassing the internationally successful *Tropa de Elite 2*, a story about an elite police squad. Behind these impressive figures there is some cause for suspicion, however: many of the preview screenings were sold out, but the cinemas weren't necessarily full, the empty seats being down to the many people who were given free tickets by the church and who then failed to turn up, so creating an inflated impression of success. The church's response to such accusations always followed the same lines: it was 'fake news' fuelled by the 'media who refuse to accept the incredible

success of films with spiritual themes in Brazil and who are trying to diminish the significance of the phenomenon'. It's true that supposedly sold-out screenings were not actually full, though; I saw it with my own eyes.

Bishop Edir Macedo and his acolytes, however, are right on one count: the Universal Church has a stormy relationship with the secular press. In 2007 the largest newspaper in the country, the *Folha de S. Paulo*, invoked the wrath of the Universal Church with a report on the business backgrounds of the leaders of the thirty-year-old organisation. Over three decades its top-ranking members had amassed between them twenty-three television channels and forty radio stations as well as nineteen other companies across various sectors, including travel agents, newspapers, a publishing house, estate agents, even an air-taxi company, Alliance Jet.

A decade later the author of the report, Elvira Lobato, published an article in the same paper about the piece that had landed her the Esso Prize (the Brazilian Pulitzer) – and a massive headache. The Universal Church had mobilised its followers and pastors to file 111 lawsuits against her and the newspaper; it tried to claim moral damages without actually contesting any of the information within the text. 'I've done TV and newspaper interviews in various countries, and I'm still asked about how the episode was a threat to the freedom of the press. The newspaper was forced to defend itself in simultaneous lawsuits in remote places, which made the defence process difficult and onerous,' she said.

The main battle is with the Globo group, which owns the largest television network in Brazil and which has already dealt a few blows to the church owned by their rival Record (for more on Globo see 'Prime Time' on page 57). In 1995 a dissident bishop leaked a video showing Edir Macedo teaching colleagues how to persuade worshippers to part with their money. In it he kneels down to count the tithe collected, spreading the bank-notes out on the floor. Looking up at the camera, he sticks his tongue out and smiles. The footage found its way to Globo. In the film biopic of his life Macedo gave his own account of the episode: they were only low-denomination notes, and the leader of the Universal Church was counting out the money on the floor because they were unable to afford a table. It all went towards paying the church's rent so that they could continue to spread the word of God.

Another episode that received wide-spread media coverage was when the bishop was detained in 1992. He was leaving a service in a green Volkswagen Santana with his wife and seventeen-year-old daughter when cars pulled up along-side them and armed men surrounded the vehicle and took him to prison. Instead of looking like a cornered outlaw as his enemies had hoped, Macedo emerged from the episode triumphant. That's his version of the story at least, faithfully conveyed in the film: in a Brazil that was just starting to see the rise of the evangeli-cals, the success of the Universal Church was a thorn in the side of those in power. One Catholic bishop openly conspired with the communications minister to topple it. They attempted to shut it down through accusations of faith healing, charlatanism and embezzlement.

THE NEO-PENTECOSTALS

The Igreja Universal do Reino de Deus, the Universal Church of the Kingdom of God, belongs to the neo-Pentecostal movement, defined as the Third Wave of Pentecostalism. Like traditional Pentecostalism, it is based on renewal and the belief that God is present and actively participating in our lives. The faithful are in direct contact with the Holy Spirit, which is called upon to fight evil, bad people and illness. They appeal to the Spirit in search of prosperity or because they want a new house, car or job. God is there to provide happiness, to set your life on the right track. Unlike the Catholic God, he is a God who operates in the here and now rather than delaying the appointment until the afterlife. This is why Pentecostal communities are found among the poorest sections of society and are widespread in Africa, Asia and South America. Data from the Brazilian Institute of Geography and Statistics show that between 1970 and 2010 the percentage of Protestants in Brazil (all categorised in the country's official census as evangélicos), a large proportion of whom are Pentecostals, grew from 5.2 to 22.2 per cent, which is a massive leap (over the same period the number of Catholics plummeted from 91.8 to 64.6 per cent). And yet the Pentecostals do not just target the disadvantaged: the Bola de Neve Church, founded in São Paulo in 1999 by a former marketing expert, Apóstolo Rina, caters to a young, middle-class audience who love to surf and skate – the altar in its church-headquarters is a surfboard. The Bola de Neve does not require adherence to any set of customs or behaviours – in fact, its popularity lies precisely in its informal approach, and it reaches out to those who have had difficulties and are in search of a new start.

Above: An evangelical preacher
speaks to his audience in Praça da
Sé – one of the areas of São Paulo
with the highest concentration of
homeless people and drug addicts
– while a homeless man **(right)**
is overcome with emotion as
he listens.

THE PASSENGER   Anna Virginia Balloussier

An evangelical group on the streets
of central São Paulo praying with
the homeless. The group meets every
Tuesday on the same corner opposite
the Municipal Theatre, handing out
food and clothes to people living
on the streets.

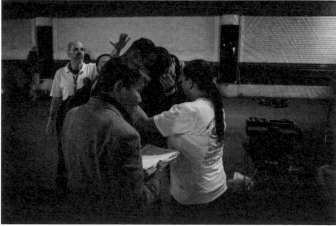

According to an article in the newspaper *O Globo*, a new evangelical church is set up in Brazil every hour: all you need is a garage, a wooden shack, a shop or a kiosk to host an assembly of believers and their pastor. But what stands out is not so much the huge number of these churches as their names. Here are a few examples: Igreja Evangélica Jesus É o Comandante (Jesus Is the Commander Evangelical Church); Igreja Pentecostal Esconderijo do Altíssimo (Hideaway of the Almighty Pentecostal Church); Assemblea Águas que Jorram do Trono de Deus (Waters that Spurt from the Throne of God Assembly); Casa de Oração Pentecostal dos Afastados (Pentecostal House of Prayer of the Strayed); Igreja a Gosto de Deus (Church to the Taste of God); Assemblea de Deus Pavio que Fumega (Smouldering Wick Assembly of God); Igreja Cuspe de Cristo (Spittle of Christ Church); Associação Evangélica Fiel Até Debaixo d'Água (Evangelical Association of the Faithful Even Underwater); Igreja Bailarinas da Valsa Divina (Dancers of the Divine Waltz Church); Igreja Batista Brasileira dos Povos Agarrados à Bíblia (Brazilian Baptist Church of the Peoples Clinging to the Bible); Comunidade do Coração Reciclado (Community of the Recycled Heart). The names are found on websites catering to the faithful and do not necessarily all actually exist, but, since we're talking about faith, why not believe in them? If nothing else, the inventiveness of the names illustrates Brazilians' imagination when thinking about God.

In his biography the bishop reveals that he 'was fine' in the crowded prison cell and was only occasionally stepped on by his fellow detainees in the rush to the toilet. But if anyone knows marketing, it's him. He summoned the press to the prison and allowed himself to be photographed behind bars, sitting on a bench with his legs crossed and chin in his hand like Rodin's sculpture *The Thinker*, reading a copy of the Bible. He left prison after eleven days to a rapturous reception from his people.

Today the Universal Church runs countless projects in Brazil and abroad. 'There is a growing demand among evangelicals in other denominations for services and practices involving prosperity theology. This is based on the claim that you can obtain blessings and material wealth if you are disciplined in your behaviour on earth. The payment of the tithe is the key component in this system, part of the bargain upheld between the human and the sacred,' says Professor Cunha.

The church's strategy for expansion involves coordinated actions, from increasing the number of its members in Brazil's National Congress to extensive investment in the mystical through services and advertising campaigns. This includes offering 24/7 contact with followers using online and in-person social networks. The Universal Church has even created a prayer 'drive-thru'. 'Do you have a minute for God?' says a sign inviting members to pray in their vehicles in the garage at the temple in São Paulo.

For a long time Edir Macedo has been preaching that evangelicals should engage with politics. In his 2008 book *Plano de Poder* ('Plan for Power') he cautions against the 'noxious' inertia of the Christian electorate, which is in part caused by an 'erroneous interpretation that God will do everything without the individual having to lift a finger'. The bishop writes: 'Machiavelli defined [politics] as "the art of governing and establishing power". If that is the case, from God's point of view, who do you think he would want to have all this power and dominion? Would he want it to be in the hands of his people or not?'

His group's first major political victory came in 2016 with the election of his nephew Marcelo Crivella, a bishop who trained at the Universal Church, to the office of mayor of Rio de Janeiro. Crivella attracted international media attention at Brazil's largest literary event, the Bienal do Livro, when he ordered the confiscation of a comic book featuring two male Marvel superheroes kissing, both fully clothed. The move, which was overturned by Brazil's Supreme Court, was a confirmation of the homophobia common in the discourse of various evangelical leaders. A week after the censorship attempt the mayor told me he had made the decision not because of the kiss but because of the dialogue, which in his view offended Brazil's Statute of the Child and Adolescent (which says nothing about homosexual relationships, only eroticised content). Part of the speech from the comic strip that alarmed Crivella included a young man who, according to him, uttered the phrase 'shake your ass' – the dialogue, in fact, contains a Portuguese expression meaning something closer to 'move your ass' in English.

His uncle deviates from this trend, which is proof of the multi-faceted nature of the evangelical sector in Brazil. A few years ago, during a radio show called *Palavra Amiga* – broadcast by the Rede Aleluia, which brings together the radio stations of the Universal Church – the bishop said, 'Many believers, pastors and churches are railing against the gay movement, against gay marriage. I ask you, would Jesus do this if he were alive today? I don't think he would. Because homosexuals existed in Jesus' time, and he didn't say anything against them. He didn't raise a banner saying: "Hey, you should preach against homosexuality and say it's not allowed, don't do it."'

That same year he was awarded the Pink Triangle prize by a major local LGBTQ group. The organisation refers to the prize as the 'gay Oscars', reappropriating the symbol used by the Nazis in concentration camps to identify homosexual inmates and which was later adopted by the community as a symbol of gay pride.

It's all relative, of course. How willing will the Universal Church be to accept LGBTQ members? According to sceptics, there is no evidence of any pastor or bishop within the church being openly gay. And Macedo was criticised years earlier for leading, whip in hand, what appeared to be an exorcism of a young gay man. But the evangelical media's friendlier attitude to LGBTQ worshippers may well be a sign of how adaptable the bishop is to modern times. As experts both inside and outside the sector point out, he may well be keeping an eye on a niche market – there's no shortage of gay people with high purchasing power, many of them without children to support, who could offer plenty of cash to the church and have yet to be embraced by other Christian denominations, whether it's the Catholics or their evangelical rivals.

After all, for the Universal Church, it's all about prosperity now. 🕊

In Defence of Fragmentation

How can we define the indefinable?
Is it possible to pin a single label
on a country so multi-faceted that
it appears almost schizophrenic?

Michel Laub

Translated by Laura Garmeson

93

The singer and composer João Gilberto is regarded as the father of bossa nova – perhaps the style of Brazilian music that has, over the past sixty years, had the highest international profile – but he was much more than that. When he passed away in July 2019 at the age of eighty-eight the majority of the obituaries lamented the end of a kind of national utopia represented by his work. The critic Lorenzo Mammi, an Italian based in Brazil who is one of the most meticulous scholars of Gilberto's oeuvre, places him alongside architect Oscar Niemeyer and footballer Pelé as one of a triumvirate who founded the belief in what he describes as a 'modernity that was fluid, light and simultaneously complex', an authentically Brazilian future, which in the late 1950s and early 1960s still seemed possible.

In political terms, the truth is that this future may only ever have existed in the dreams of a section of the enlightened middle classes, dreams which were crushed by the 1964 military coup. In cultural terms, it was a yearning that was confined to the fields of music, architecture and football – and possibly the margins of cinema, theatre and sociology. When it comes to literature, Brazil has never had much belief in an optimistic self-image. Even in the very best of its aesthetic expression our poetry has no equivalent to a Virgil celebrating the might of the Roman Empire or a Walt Whitman with his faith in the triumphant values of American democracy. Modern writers tend to be drawn more to the negative, the awareness of a culture's aesthetic, political and moral paradoxes. And the greatest writers Brazil has produced are creatures of modernity. In poetry, Carlos Drummond de Andrade, who

MICHEL LAUB (pictured right) is a Brazilian writer and journalist who graduated in law but abandoned a career as a lawyer to move to São Paulo and devote himself to writing. He has published collections of short stories and novels: *Diário da Queda* (2011), published in English as *Diary of the Fall* (Harvill Secker USA/Vintage UK, 2014), has been translated into numerous languages and been awarded prizes including the Brazilian Literature Award and the Prêmio Bravo.

oscillated between political engagement and a certain existentialist scepticism, and João Cabral de Melo Neto, with his formal rigour and arid themes and sensibility, could never be mistaken for celebratory artists.

It is the same in prose. Machado de Assis used irony against the colonial and aristocratic society of Rio de Janeiro in the late 19th century; in the 1930s and 1940s Graciliano Ramos wrote a socially engaged novel that was acutely aware of the urban and rural contradictions of the Brazilian Northeast; in the 1950s Guimarães Rosa described a *sertão* in Minas Gerais that was as epic and mythical as it was poor and brutal; from the middle to the second half of the 20th century Nelson Rodrigues and Clarice Lispector saw turmoil in the individual soul to rival that of the grand sweep of history.

Around the time of João Gilberto, who established his signature style with the release of his debut album *Chega de Saudade* in 1959, there was already a notable difference between the smooth harmonies of bossa nova, associated with a political idea of conciliation – the sweet common denominator capable of uniting all sections of society – and the decidedly thornier edges of Brazilian literature. In 1963 Rubem Fonseca published his debut short-story collection *Os Prisioneiros*. The book seemed out of place at the time – during that period of the 20th century when Brazil was at its richest, between post-Second World War economic prosperity and the outbreak of the Cold War in Latin America – in its portrayal of a country that was fragmented, authoritarian and violent with a level of urban and social disintegration without precedent in our literary tradition. During the twenty-year dictatorship, and even after the return to democracy in 1985 – which, with a few ups and downs, has lasted to the present day – the Brazilian fictional imagination bears closer resemblance to that of Rubem Fonseca than bossa nova. You can see this in the themes and approaches of the writers from this period and in the kinds of debates that were sparked by their major works.

There is one aspect that might seem normal to us today but which up until the late 20th century would have sounded like alienated particularism. Since independence in 1822 Brazil has been a country in search of an identity: in a former colony that is at once modern and archaic, urban and rural, syncretic and exclusive, with a population made up of indigenous people, ex-slaves and European immigrants, it has always been difficult to find common ground on which to base any kind of unifying theory of national character. Contrary to what sociologists and politicians have attempted to achieve, literature gave up trying to 'define Brazil' – in a serious way at least – in the 1980s. Up to that point, from the romanticism of the 19th century through to modernism and the work of authors such as Jorge Amado, this was still a viable aesthetic project. Since the 1980s, however, our poetry and prose have reflected the same awareness of fragmentation that can be found in Fonseca's work. There is as much that is 'Brazilian' in the regionalist themes of the novels of Ana Miranda as there is in the universalism of Bernardo Carvalho. The same is true for a poet with Catholic influences like Adélia Prado and a gay short-story writer like Caio Fernando Abreu. In terms of form, literary production from this period owes as much to the classical frameworks of the canon as the authors who have worked to push the boundaries of narrative experimentation, including Dalton Trevisan, Sérgio Sant'Ana and Valêncio Xavier.

In this lack of definition – which is in itself a definition – emerging alongside a historic process of democratising access to education (or, at least, to information, which is a step in the

right direction), it is only natural that a space should open up for voices that diverge from the typical model of stories told by or about white middle-class authors, usually men. One milestone in this reversal was the novel *Cidade de Deus* (1997; English title *City of God*) by Paulo Lins, which attracted global attention thanks to the prize-winning 2002 film adaptation by directors Fernando Meirelles and Kátia Lund. Others included the rehabilitation of the work of Carolina de Jesus, a black woman and refuse collector from the 1960s, or the affirmation of names like Ana Maria Gonçalves and Conceição Evaristo, both of whom were also black, and Geovani Martins and Ferréz who, like Paulo Lins, are rare examples of writers who come from the periphery or the *favela*.

Aesthetics and sociology coexist within contemporary Brazilian literature, as in all countries. Literary prizes are one possible means of gauging what is being read and – if we're fortunate enough to have good judging panels – discovering the most vibrant and relevant new writing, and they have been reflecting this diversity of voices and themes. Some of the young (or young at the time) prize-winners from the past two decades include Luiz Ruffato (see 'An Author Recommends' on page 200), who has built an entire body of work on the private lives of a working-class community in Minas Gerais; Ana Paula Maia, who writes about violence in the Baixada Fluminense in Rio; Ana Martins Marques, a poet with a delicate eye and a keen sense for the subtleties of daily life; and Julián Fuks, who writes about the repercussions of the military dictatorships in Argentina and Brazil as the son of immigrants who fled the former country for the latter.

In terms of the most recent literary offerings, it is difficult to group Brazilian fiction under any single banner or along any clear lines of theme, style or approach. I have picked out two books by authors with a certain depth of experience that are sufficiently different from one another on these metrics. These are: *Noite Dentro da Noite* (2017) by Joca Terron, a long, ambitious and vibrant novel that uses memory, political reflection and fantastical elements to describe the author's childhood in the Pantanal region of Mato Grosso along with episodes from the Second World War and the Brazilian military dictatorship; and *Marrom e Amarelo* (2019) by Paulo Scott, a short and intense piece of fiction about two brothers, born of a black father and a white mother, who live in a violent neighbourhood in Porto Alegre – the narrator, who is seen as white during his turbulent adolescence in the 1980s, becomes a political activist and gets involved in a plot that leads him to relive episodes of the racism he witnessed involving his brother, who is black.

When João Gilberto died, the general mourning was heightened in part because it coincided with the first year of the presidency of Jair Bolsonaro. In the case of literature, however, there is no nostalgia for a paradise lost. The contrast between the brutality in power today and the country's literary production is of a different nature: alongside new writing from well-known authors independent publishers have been doing the important work of raising awareness of voices outside the official circuit, in prose and poetry alike, with a whole network of evening talks, workshops, small events and festivals that are enacting resistance in these times of economic hardship and when the crack-down on the cultural sector has already begun. The mere fact that this flurry of activity exists helps to keep the darkness at bay and serves as a source of potential optimism that, who knows, might just transcend the world of aesthetics to become real life. 🐦

THE R

STEPHANIE NOLEN

A scene near the Samuel hydroelectric power plant, close to Porto Velho, Rondônia; this controversial project has had a severe impact on the environment and releases more greenhouse gases than an oil-fired plant when in operation.

OAD

Highway BR-163 cuts a brutal path through Brazil's conflicting ambitions: to transform itself into an economic powerhouse and to preserve the Amazon as a bulwark against climate change. Stephanie Nolen travelled two thousand kilometres along the dusty, dangerous corridor and found a range of realistic – and often counter-intuitive – ways that the forest could work for everyone.

Every single day cameras on satellites seven hundred kilometres above the Earth sweep over the five million square kilometres of Amazon rainforest in Brazil and record a series of images. The pictures show the soaring trees that spike above the canopy and the tangle of jungle below, threaded through with rivers, some swift and muddy brown, others nearly as green as the sea of trees. They show the cities and the towns and the indigenous *aldeias* that are home to the thirty million people who live within the forest. And the pictures show the fires that rage across the Amazon, the bare patches of charred ground, the gouged raw earth of the mines, the speckled sprawl of hectares of grazing cattle and the fresh scars where trees stood yesterday and have disappeared today. As the satellites pass over the forest, they record its disappearance in real time.

Brazil began to collect these images (on satellites belonging to NASA, China and India) in 2004, a key part of the country's big push to stop the burning and the gouging. The pictures are sent to teams of field agents who head to the sites of fires and patches of newly denuded land to make arrests, levy fines and destroy the equipment of loggers and miners and those who cleared the land for ranches and farms.

And it worked. Between 2004 and 2014 Brazil drove deforestation down by 82 per cent. The early pictures photographed the forest at a resolution that showed the land in 25-hectare blocks, and so those who cleared it started to strip out smaller patches, hoping to elude the satellites. Over time, Brazil's Ministry of Environment and the Brazilian Space Agency developed a new camera that zoomed in to capture images as precise as a single hectare. Deforestation rates fell further.

Yet the forest was still disappearing. A chunk bigger than Montenegro vanished in 2018. And when I set out to try to understand why – and what that means not just for Brazil but for the rest of us humans – the most knowledgeable people I talked with seemed to be filled with a level of despair I had never before encountered when reporting on climate issues. Again and again scientists told me that the future of the forest had never been as uncertain as it is right now.

The satellites give a constant picture of what's happening in the Amazon. But there is a limit to what you can learn from the sky. You can't hear the voices of the

STEPHANIE NOLEN has worked as a correspondent in more than eighty countries, reporting from Africa, India and Latin America for Canadian national newspaper *The Globe and Mail*. A seven-time winner at the Canada National Newspaper Awards and the Amnesty International Media Awards, she focuses mainly on equality and social inclusion, war, health and malnutrition. Her book *28: Stories of Aids in Africa* (Knopf Canada, 2007) won her the PEN Courage Award in 2007.

people who live in the Amazon and who see their own future, and Brazil's, tied to how they use the forest every day. You can't see those who feel they have a stake in – and a right to – the wealth that the rainforest holds. And you certainly can't feel the taut, maybe irresolvable, tension between all their many and conflicting visions.

To try to understand how we reached this moment, I drew up a list of the many actors involved and the multiple forces that seemed to have coalesced to get us here. Then I laid out a map of Brazil and traced the borders of the remaining forest. I noticed a road, the BR-163, that seemed as if it might help me see the whole story. From the air, the Amazon is, still, predominantly a sea of trees. On the roads that cut through it, it's something else entirely.

1. HIGHWAY OF AMBITIONS

The sky was a flat grey when Elisângela Mendonça, a producer in the Rio bureau of the Canadian newspaper *The Globe and Mail*, and photographer Aaron Elkaim and I set out on our first morning, the sun obscured by the haze of fires burning to the north.

We hit the road – steering a silver Chevy pickup truck on a journey that would take us more than two thousand kilometres through the Amazon. Heading into the smoke, we left behind the boxy white highrises and wide boulevards of the business district of • CUIABÁ, the capital of Brazil's agro-industrial heartland. We slotted our pickup truck into a giant line of eighteen-wheelers hauling grain, all rendered the same taupe colour by caked dust.

The road is a smooth dual-carriageway when it leaves the city, with paved shoulders and occasional tollbooths, the kind of highway you'd expect to find carving its way through a modern agricultural superpower.

It doesn't last.

The story of this road, the BR-163, is in many ways the story of Brazil's relationship with the rainforest. When construction of the highway began back in 1972, the country was ruled by a dictatorship that viewed the Amazon as a risk: all that unoccupied territory, ripe for the taking by an enemy. And so the military rulers devised a policy, *integrar para não entregar* – integrate so we don't lose it – that aimed to move more people into the forest, fast. In the process of marking Brazilian ownership of the Amazon, the military rulers were also able to achieve another critical goal: the resettlement of poor, landless people who were then swelling the cities of Rio de Janeiro and São Paulo searching for work. This road, the BR-163, was a key north–south pole in that expansion.

Today it runs from Cuiabá, in the heart of the grain basket, to Santarém, a muggy port city on the Amazon River. As it snakes north it cuts a path not only through the country itself but through Brazil's conflicting ambitions: to transform itself into a first-world economy on the one hand, and, on the other, to protect and preserve what is left of an ecosystem that recycles a fifth of the world's rainfall, holds 150 billion tonnes of stored carbon and is home to 15 per cent of all the species on Earth.

On both sides of the highway were fields – vast expanses stubbled with the remains of harvested corn and soya. Every ten minutes or so we drove past a little clump of trees – preserved by a farmer to shade a house or cover a water source – and roughly every fifty kilometres past a grain-storage facility, its silos and ramps and trucks all so big that it felt like we were in *Alice's Adventures in Wonderland*, suddenly shrunk.

The outsize scale of the farms and the trucks was fitting, given what this region

BR-163

CUIABÁ •

represents for Brazil. The government adapted soya plants for this climate in the 1970s, and farmers began to move here from the south. But in the past fifteen years, as global demand exploded – primarily for soya to use in animal feed and for livestock to nourish a new middle class in China and other emerging economies – the wealth and the political importance of this area began to grow. Soya products accounted for $27 billion in exports in 2017. As Brazil has lived through its worst recession in nearly a century, this was one sector that continued to expand. That gave farmers and landowners, always a strong political force here, an even greater influence.

For the last forty-five years the southern border of the forest has been pushed steadily back. From the time of the generals and into the 1990s this was explicit government policy. The transition to democracy came just as domestic and international pressure about preserving the rainforest began to mount. Brazil took a new tack, saying it would try to control deforestation – assisted by an international fund, backed primarily by Norway, that recognised that the country was being asked to preserve forest cover of the kind that rich nations had demolished in their own path to development.

Then came an interesting confluence of events that complicated Brazil's relationship with deforestation. In 2002 Luiz Inácio Lula da Silva, known as Lula, was elected Brazil's president. His first years in office coincided with a surge in global commodity prices that made Brazil richer and Lula popular – and fuelled a surge in forest clearing to make way for cattle and • SOYA, much of it shipped to world markets along the BR-163. Lula was sensitive to the international criticism about the Amazon, and he tasked his environment

minister with sorting it out. Marina Silva, a protégée of the assassinated environmental activist Chico Mendes, drew up a transformative plan to change the way Brazil managed its forest. The key was robust police enforcement, employing those satellite images. For the tricky issue of Amazon highways, she put forward a plan called the Sustainable BR-163, which proposed the road be used to enable development but be carefully managed to control deforestation. A key measure involved turning huge areas of land along the road into Conservation Units, removing them from the land-speculation market.

Ms Silva eventually quit the cabinet, disillusioned, but her plan was tremendously successful. Deforestation fell by 58 per cent during her time as minister. Brazil continued to lose, on average, 9,600 square kilometres of the forest, an area the size of Cyprus, annually – but the downward trend, even as GDP and income rose, was a powerful endorsement of sustainable resource management.

Yet, starting in 2014 – as political turmoil and corruption scandals engulfed Brazil – deforestation rates suddenly shot up again, likely a result of the perception that there would be few repercussions for breaking the law. Dilma Rousseff, Lula's hand-picked successor, was impeached in 2016 after six years in power and replaced by her vice-president, Michel Temer, a long-time patron of rich landowners, soya farmers and ranchers. Mr Temer himself was soon ensnared in scandal and turned to those *ruralistas* to ensure his survival by proposing to ease restrictions on everything from mining to ranching in protected forest. 'All of the gains we had made in the past thirty years, creating environmental safeguards, laws that organise land occupation, are being exchanged with this rural elite. They're

BR-163

CUIABÁ

'These political, economic and social conflicts are braided together in Brazil, and the BR-163 runs right through them: a dusty, dangerous corridor to prosperity – or destruction.'

the bargaining chip to keep Temer as president,' Ane Alencar told me before the road trip. She's a scientist who helped write the plan for the Sustainable BR-163 and a co-founder of the Amazon Environmental Research Institute.

Deforestation surged under Temer – and then Brazilian politics took another twist that put the Amazon at even greater risk. Frustration with Temer, Lula and the traditional political class helped propel a far-right populist named Jair Bolsonaro into the presidency in late 2018. He decried forest protection as a waste of Brazil's resources, said racist things about indigenous people and mocked their land claims and said no other nation should have a voice in how the Amazon was managed. He had the enthusiastic support of agro-industry, which donated generously to his campaign. Once he was in office he moved quickly to repay them. He slashed the funding for forest monitoring, abolished the autonomous indigenous-affairs agency that had regulated and protected vast chunks of the Amazon for its original inhabitants, fired the head of the space agency that did the satellite monitoring after he released data showing a spike in clearances and tried to abolish the Ministry of the Environment altogether

(that last step was a bit too much even for the ruralist-dominated Congress). In mid-2019 the result was the Amazon's worst ever season of burning, as emboldened land-grabbers and farmers moved to put new land under till, knowing they would face no consequences. The data for January 2020, when Bolsonaro had been in office a year, showed an 85 per cent increase in deforestation over the rate the year before.

These political, economic and social conflicts are braided together in Brazil, and the BR-163 runs right through them: a dusty, dangerous corridor to prosperity – or destruction, depending on whom you ask.

2. 'THE WORLD NEEDS FOOD'

A few kilometres before the town of Sinop we turned off on to a red-dirt road and an hour later pulled up in front of the farm office of Darcy Ferrarin, a wiry, blue-eyed farmer of seventy-two whose Portuguese is still marked with the round vowels of the far south where he grew up. Mr Ferrarin bought this 13,300-hectare farm, called St Mary of the Amazon, in 1998; it's one of four he owns, worth collectively about $4 million.

Here, too, there are vast fields, recently harvested. But there are trees as well: more than a third of Mr Ferrarin's land – 5,300 hectares – remains primary-growth tropical forest. It is not because he is a bleeding-heart environmentalist, he was at pains to make clear, that he has preserved those trees. He believes the government will eventually pay out to reward those who protect the forest cover; in the meantime, the trees help keep his

Pages 108–9: A FUNAI (indigenous-affairs agency) helicopter takes off during operations to fight fires in the Amazon rainforest that have been started deliberately.

In today's world, soya can be compared with oil, except that instead of powering cars it provides fuel for cows, chickens and, above all, pigs. As pork production has grown exponentially, driven in large part by the needs of China, which consumes billions of pigs a year (although Europe is a serious consumer, too), soya cultivation has required ever more space. South America is the new Eldorado: Brazil, Argentina and Paraguay between them produce half the world's soya. In Brazil, soya monoculture has sparked a new colonialism, both on the part of Brazilian producers and the major global producers, who are going after the only remaining free space: Amazonia. Livestock farms have grown, gobbling up side orders of forest, but the expansion has come mainly from crop cultivation. The climate is ideal: warm and wet all year round. According to environmental group Greenpeace, soya cultivation takes up thirty-three million hectares in Brazil (half the size of France), and much of this land is located in the belt to the south of the great forest. Monoculture is advancing thanks to the fertilisers and pesticides legalised by Bolsonaro; these are toxic to the environment and local family farming, which is being destroyed along with the forest. Travelling down the well-maintained roads, you have to imagine that the hundreds of miles of peaceful soya plants, all future animal protein, were once biodiverse landscapes and home to rural populations. Timber, meat and soya have combined in a lethal scheme that is conspiring against the future of the world's largest tropical rainforest and the stability of our climate.

water sources running. He believes that farmers like him should be compensated through a global fund for the trees they leave standing.

But not all of them. 'I'm not in favour of zero deforestation – I'm in favour of legal deforestation,' he says. 'The world needs food. No one can live from forest.' And Brazil needs the exports. 'Agribusiness,' he says, 'is what's keeping this country afloat.'

Under Brazil's Forest Code the owners of land in the Amazon can clear only 20 per cent of their property; the balance they must preserve or restore to forest if it was previously cleared. There was an amnesty when the code was brought in in 2012, which is how Mr Ferrarin gets away with having less than that. Besides, he is disputing whether his forest technically would be Amazon, claiming he is in the transition zone from a savannah-like biome called the *cerrado*, an argument that has been embraced by environmental authorities under Mr Bolsonaro.

Despite its quaint name, this farm is an unabashedly industrialised operation. There is a factory right on the property, where freshly picked cotton is processed and bound into pallets headed to Asia.

Standing in the clatter of the factory, I recalled a conversation I'd had with Juliano Assunção, a prominent economist who heads a think tank in Rio called the Climate Policy Initiative. Farms such as this stand on what used to be forest, sure, but as highly efficient, industrialised operations, he said, they also represent part of the solution for the Amazon.

'I know that miles upon miles of soya fields are quite shocking, and they look like a much more devastated environment than having a few cows grazing in among trees,' Mr Assunção said, 'but the soya industry has made huge productivity gains over the past few decades, and in doing so has allowed farmers to get more out of less land.'

What's more, farmers such as Mr Ferrarin have made considerable investment in their land, which means they have more to lose by not complying with the law. That makes them more transparent, more accountable and more influenced by consumer demands for a 'green' supply chain, he said. If such farmers stick within the existing boundaries of land they are permitted to clear and focus on the most efficient agriculture possible within that area, they are potentially part of the solution.

Brazil, he was saying, needs more Mr Ferrarins – and less of what lay ahead of us as we drove further north to our next stop.

3. PRIDE – AND A CONFESSION

The road to Fazenda Esperança, Hope Farm, was hard to find. We travelled east from the BR-163 and blundered down a few smaller roads – encountering a perplexed armadillo and a pair of men skinning an enormous, freshly killed cow. Gesturing expansively with machetes that dripped blood, they gave us friendly but entirely inaccurate directions. Eventually we found the unmarked entrance to the • FARM and parked our truck by a field of bulls penned up awaiting a slaughterhouse truck.

Invaldo Weiss, sixty-one, strode out to greet us, immaculate in lustrous cowboy boots, jeans with a stiff crease ironed in and a smart cotton shirt. His pride was evident as he drove us around the ranch. He, too, came from the south, some forty years ago, in the early days of Amazonian colonisation. He built Esperança by acquiring a series of small properties. 'When I bought it I had to clean up the rest of the native vegetation,' he said in Portuguese. By *limpar*, clean, he meant cut down. He stopped the truck at one point to show us

a clump of three grand trees. 'I left those,' he said proudly. A shifting, tail-swishing clump of cattle stood beneath it, each trying to keep within the small circle of shade the trees cast.

There are twice as many cows as there are people in Brazil – but this country has the world's least productive cattle industry. In Canada, for example, farmers raise, on average, seven cows per hectare; here, they raise just one. Forging new pasture for cattle is the single biggest driver of deforestation – responsible for 66 per cent of it. But that statistic can be deceiving. Often it isn't the push to graze more cattle that drives farmers to fell trees. Instead, cattle are used to declare de facto ownership of land that has been purchased or occupied. Brazil's land-titling system is intensely bureaucratic, extremely slow and often simply absent; just 30 per cent of landowners in the state of Pará, where we were headed, have legal title to their land. And because people who don't have title to land can't rent it out – or sell it – keeping cattle makes it productive without anyone having to do much: Brazil's cattle are turned loose in fields of scrubby vegetation and left for weeks at a time under minimal supervision.

Mr Weiss showed us humpbacked bulls mottled in browns and blacks, raised for semen, and grey cows who eyed us suspiciously, edging between us and their tiny newborn calves that glowed white against the brittle grass.

He told us about his part-time role as an evangelical pastor. He told us how proud he was of his daughters, both college graduates – he never had the chance to go past junior school. His children are raising their own families in the town of Sinop. And after we had been talking for several hours, and the harsh lines of the pastures had softened in the

Pages 114–15: The settlement of Vila Nova Samuel – which grew up with the arrival of migrants from all across the country to build the dam for the Samuel HEP plant – survives on legal and illegal deforestation of the Amazon rainforest.

late-afternoon light, Mr Weiss chuckled and offered to 'confess'. When first he came north he made a living by operating heavy machinery, he said, and then he saved up enough to buy the equipment himself and began to hire himself out to clear farmland: two tractors and a chain slung between them – that's how the fifty-metre trees of the Amazon were brought down. And that's how he made the money to acquire Esperança.

He quit clearing in 2005, when the government's new regime of enforcement kicked in. 'I never did any work without documents, nothing illegal,' he said. The top environmental official in the region was a friend of his and warned him he could end up behind bars if he cleared land for people with fake permits. 'So I got out of the business – other people went on working on whatever terms.'

Not that Mr Weiss was opposed to a little creative sidestepping of the law once he became a farmer. When warnings began piling up that he wasn't meeting his obligations to replant the cleared areas of his property, he took a stack of them into the office of his pal and dumped them on his desk. They had a gentleman's agreement that the warnings and fines would 'go away', he said, and he has simply ignored them for years.

But what about his cattle business? In 2009 Brazil won a commitment from major beef producers that they would not purchase cattle raised on illegally deforested land. But Mr Weiss said with a shrug that he has no trouble selling his animals. He does not have formal registration of his property; to get it he would have to reforest, something he has no intention of doing. 'It's not my responsibility.' He is focused instead on modernising his ranch – he's building up from three cows per hectare to six – and he is converting some pasture to soya fields.

The environmental lobby drives him bonkers. The stars of Brazilian soap operas are always collecting signatures on petitions to preserve the forest, he said, without thinking for a minute about where their food comes from. 'They won't pay a penny to reforest. I'm the one whose pocket it's supposed to come from ... I came here and built something, and now I'm the villain.'

We left Mr Weiss at nightfall and headed north to Sinop. The number of trucks on the road was beginning to thin; some were pulled over, their drivers fixing dinner on a small pop-down shelf on the side of the truck bed.

We spent the night in Sinop – another fast-expanding city where the most conspicuous evidence of new prosperity is private schools and late-model pick-ups. Driving out early the next morning we passed a long string of warehouses, grain-processing centres and abattoirs – with signs in Chinese and Japanese as well as Portuguese – and a shiny new airport. A long, sketchy stretch of road lay between us and the regional capital, Novo Progresso.

4. THE GOLD FACTOR

Here, the site of some of Brazil's most violent conflicts over land and resources, we wanted to meet up with a team of agents from the Chico Mendes Institute for the Conservation of Biodiversity (ICMBio). We drove out of Novo Progresso just after dawn, carrying with us the latest satellite images and GPS devices, joining a convoy of six truckloads of agents backed up by a dozen heavily armed forest police.

At midday we pulled up to a skeletal shed in the middle of Jamanxim National Forest. The ICMBio agents leaped down from their pickups and homed in on four men sitting out the heavy midday heat under the rough metal roof, while the police fanned out to form a semi-circular perimeter.

The men were cooking beans on a gas ring connected to a tank of propane; the blue flame hissed and the steel pot juddered. At first the rattle from the pot drowned out all the other sounds. One of the agents, Nilton Barth Filho, stepped over to the tank and turned the flame down. For a second I thought this was courtesy. If they were going to interrogate these men, they would make sure lunch didn't burn. But, as the noise died away, a second sound was audible – the drone of an engine somewhere in the forest behind us. Mr Barth Filho's head snapped up as he heard it, and then he and three colleagues bolted towards it.

The sound of the engine stayed steady – so it wasn't loggers with chainsaws. It was a pump: *garimpeiros* panning for ● GOLD. A few hundred metres into the forest was a clearing pocked with muddy pits, where the agents found three men standing waist deep in a wide, murky pool, funnelling water through a series of wooden pans. The police put their hands on their guns and summoned the miners. They came slowly, dripping silty water.

The police lined them up in a thatched hut where a row of hammocks hung. Searching the men, and the battered backpacks that held their gear, they found two repurposed eye-drop bottles – now heavy with the mercury that *garimpeiros* use to

separate gold from silt – and a rifle and some shells. A woman cooking in the hut began to weep as she watched the agents rummage through their small heap of possessions. The miners – five in all – were soon marched up to the main building, where one agent, Mila Ferreira, began the process of fining their leader, Francinaldo da Silva Lima, forty-two.

Back in the forest, mission leader Assor Fucks supervised as Mr Barth Filho and another agent, Eder de Jesus, went at the pump and the camp with sledgehammers, battering $8,000 worth of equipment into uselessness.

Drenched in sweat when the job was done, Mr Filho had a satisfied air. His team had been patrolling the forest for six hours by then, chasing false leads on cattle ranchers and loggers who always seemed to elude them. He was delighted to have made a bust.

'They do so much damage, these guys – they open up the forest, they send mercury into the streams, and it poisons everything,' he said, heading back up to his truck.

Mr Jesus watched his partner go and shook his head. '*Peixinhos*,' he muttered. '*Só peixinhos*.' Just little fish.

Both the agents were right in their way. The *garimpeiros* do drive deforestation across the Amazon, but their environmental impact is dwarfed by that of the legal mining industry, which has a large – and growing – presence in the rainforest. There are active legal mines, exploration sites or purchased concessions on almost a million square kilometres of land in the Amazon; mining in this region was worth 4 per cent of Brazil's GDP in 2016. Mines must undergo an extensive environmental licensing procedure, and companies are required to later 'restore' the area they have mined, which means the impact of

BR-163

CUIABÁ

> "'If the punishment was serious – if the law applied here ...
> Even if we had a hundred vehicles and all these people, it
> wouldn't fix it. Because it's politics.'"

mining can appear relatively small compared to farming or logging. But new research has found that mining leaves a significant footprint. Australian ecologist Laura Sonter recently demonstrated that 9 per cent of the forest loss between 2005 and 2015 was caused by mining. That's twelve times more than occurred within mining lease areas alone. The additional deforestation comes from urban areas that grow up to house the workforce, industries that expand to serve the supply chain and big infrastructure projects built to support the mine.

Mining has been prohibited in protected areas for decades, but more than five million hectares of land – equal to the size of Costa Rica – are the subject of bills before the Brazilian Congress seeking to lower their protection status to allow mining, and President Bolsonaro has said that mining in the region will play a key role in his efforts to bolster Brazil's economy. Given the scale of the industry, it was easy to understand why Mr Jesus felt that busting a few men panning for gold was pointless. But they weren't having much luck with ranchers and loggers that day either.

On missions like these, the ICMBio agents try to locate new infractions and identify who has cut down the trees that have gone missing in those satellite pictures. The Novo Progresso team of nine

agents was responsible for an area equivalent, in total, to the size of Portugal – nine million hectares of forest. 'A million each!' Mr Barth Filho told me with a somewhat manic laugh. Just a few hours into their day of patrols, it was clear how fruitless their task was. The land was rumpled with low hills and rocky outcrops, and we passed smouldering new pasture and more cattle. Deep inside the highly protected area it looked just like it did outside the conservation zone.

'The scenario is depressing,' Ms Ferreira said. 'It's very sad to see not only the absence of forest but the fires.'

When we encountered houses or farm buildings the agents stopped and interrogated any people they found. The stories were identically vague. 'I don't know who owns that land. I don't know who started the fire.'

Mr Fucks was clearly annoyed. 'Police have no resources or capacity to assist us with intelligence or investigations,' he said as he walked back to the truck after another fruitless conversation with a steadfastly evasive farmer.

'We can't get them,' Ms Ferreira chimed in, her voice flat with frustration. 'Eighty per cent of the time, we know – but we can't prove it. They put the land in someone else's name, and we issue fines, and nothing happens – they toss the fine in the drawer. The only person who ever pays the fine is a small land-grabber who is afraid of the attention.'

Landowners with outstanding fines can't get access to government credit programmes – that's one of those enforcement

Pages 118–19: Firefighters tackling a forest blaze.

measures brought in at the beginning of the turnaround period in the mid-2000s. But, for a nominal fee or the use of some land, they can easily find someone to put their name on the property. 'Brazil's problem is impunity,' said Ms Ferreira. 'If people who break the law ever got punished it wouldn't just keep happening.'

Mr Jesus chimed in. 'The only way they get punished is that we destroy their equipment, like their tractors and their pumps,' he explained – something ICMBio agents have been authorised to do since 2009 when they come upon an environmental crime. 'That,' he adds, 'is when our work gets dangerous.' A law currently before Congress, proposed by the head of the *ruralista* lobby, would bar agents from destroying equipment.

When, after hours of this, we finally encountered the *garimpo*, the agents were jittery with adrenalin. But, even as they smashed up the equipment, it was clear they weren't striking much of a blow for the forest.

Ms Ferreira spoke simply and gently as she explained the charges to Mr Lima, the head of the small group of miners; Mr Jesus helped him ink his thumb to sign the charge sheet he couldn't read.

'Did you know this was Jamanxim Forest and you can't mine here?' she asked Mr Lima.

'No,' he replied, 'I never heard that.' He was standing with one foot on an old wooden sign that identified the area as protected; he couldn't read that either.

Mr Fucks said their fruitless hours in the forest put a lie to any platitudes from government about forest protection. 'We need [more] employees and three times as many vehicles. We only have what we do because foreign governments donate them … We're losing. But if we had three times as many people we could win.'

Yet, when Ms Ferreira peeled off her bullet-proof vest at the end of the day, she questioned whether beefing up their ranks would really make a difference. The most powerful politicians in Novo Progresso, she pointed out, own the farms inside the forest. 'If the punishment was serious – if the law applied here … Even if we had a hundred vehicles and all these people, it wouldn't fix it. Because it's politics.'

5. THE POLITICS OF PROGRESS

'Would you like tea? It's *mate*. We grow it ourselves.' This was the gracious welcome from a politician at the centre of this ongoing conflict when we went to see him the next morning. At ● NOVO PROGRESSO's unpretentious single-storey city hall, we were ushered in to meet the vice-mayor, Gelson Dill. (The mayor, Ubiraci Silva, does not meet with journalists. The fact that he is facing $390,000 in fines for environmental crimes may have something to do with this.)

Mr Dill was elected to the number-two job in this municipality – which, at 38,000 square kilometres, is about the size of the land area of Switzerland – in 2017, but he has served as a municipal councillor for almost as long as he has been a farmer, because, he says, producers must have a voice in politics. He was eager to talk to us about the development challenges in the region. Trucks spent more than ten days parked on the BR-163 near the city in 2017, he said, when the rains turned the highway to mud, and the government had to airlift in supplies. Only a fifth of local producers have been able to register title to their land because the process is so slow and complicated, he complained.

I broached Mr Dill's own environmental record gingerly, but it turned out he was eager to discuss the subject. He breezily confirmed what I'd heard, that he owns

BR-163

CUIABÁ

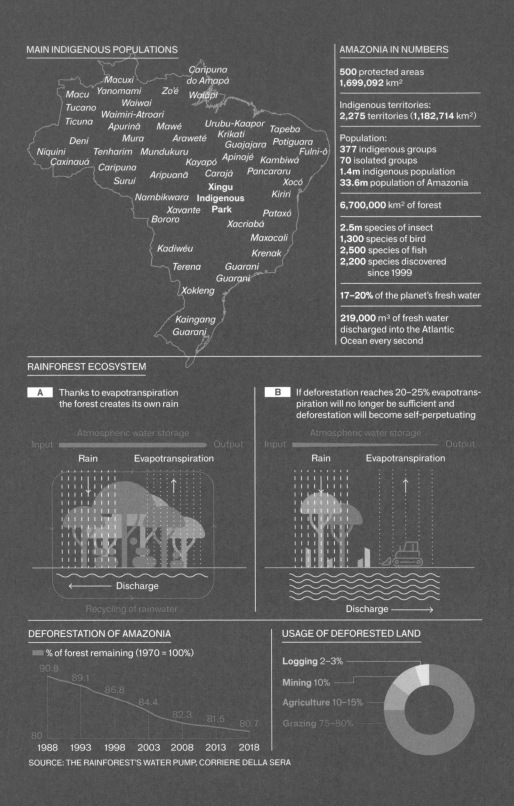

MAIN INDIGENOUS POPULATIONS

Caripuna
do Amapá
Macuxi
Macu
Yanomami
Zo'é
Walãpi
Tucano
Waiwai
Ticuna
Waimiri-Atroari
Apurinã
Mawé
Urubu-Kaapor
Tapeba
Deni
Mura
Araweté
Krikati
Potiguara
Niquini
Tenharim
Mundukuru
Guajajara
Fulni-ô
Caxinauá
Apinajé
Kambiwá
Caripuna
Kayapó
Pancararu
Suruí
Aripuanã
Carajá
Xocó
Xingu
Nambikwara
Indigenous
Kiriri
Xavante
Park
Pataxó
Bororo
Xacriabá
Maxacali
Kadiwéu
Krenak
Terena
Guarani
Guarani
Xokleng
Kaingang
Guarani

AMAZONIA IN NUMBERS

500 protected areas
1,699,092 km²

Indigenous territories:
2,275 territories (**1,182,714** km²)

Population:
377 indigenous groups
70 isolated groups
1.4m indigenous population
33.6m population of Amazonia

6,700,000 km² of forest

2.5m species of insect
1,300 species of bird
2,500 species of fish
2,200 species discovered
since 1999

17–20% of the planet's fresh water

219,000 m³ of fresh water
discharged into the Atlantic
Ocean every second

RAINFOREST ECOSYSTEM

A Thanks to evapotranspiration
the forest creates its own rain

B If deforestation reaches 20–25% evapotranspiration will no longer be sufficient and
deforestation will become self-perpetuating

Atmospheric water storage
Input — Output
Rain — Evapotranspiration
← Discharge
Recycling of rainwater

Atmospheric water storage
Input — Output
Rain — Evapotranspiration
Discharge →

DEFORESTATION OF AMAZONIA

% of forest remaining (1970 = 100%)

90.8
89.1
86.8
84.4
82.3
81.5
80.7
80

1988 1993 1998 2003 2008 2013 2018

USAGE OF DEFORESTED LAND

Logging 2–3%
Mining 10%
Agriculture 10–15%
Grazing 75–80%

SOURCE: THE RAINFOREST'S WATER PUMP, CORRIERE DELLA SERA

a farm inside Jamanxim National Forest. But he said he owned it before the land was declared a Conservation Unit and that it was part of a family enterprise in the area that included logging and sawmill businesses. The logging was rendered illegal overnight when the area was given protected status. His brothers gave up and moved, but he kept the ranch on the footprint they already occupied, he said.

The Rousseff government denied him compensation on the grounds that he had occupied the land illegally, but under the Temer administration he and the owners of the other 250 ranches in the protected forest in Novo Progresso found a newly sympathetic ear. By recategorising 400,000 of the 1.3 million hectares of the Conservation Unit, he says, the government could address the uncertain situation of 95 per cent of the people living in the protected area. The farmers are now negotiating with the new government over precisely how much land, and which areas specifically, would have its conservation status downgraded, and he said he expects the law to change soon.

Environmentalists and protection officers abhor the plan – not just for the amount of forest that would be lost within the rezoned area but for the message it would send to land-grabbers and speculators in the rest of the country: if they occupy and clear protected land and settle in, sooner or later they will be given ownership – and the right to deforest. Ms Alencar, the conservation scientist who drew up the original Sustainable BR-163 plan, put it this way to me before I set out on the drive: 'If the government says, "We will change the limits of Jamanxim National Forest and everyone that is there is allowed to be there" – imagine what will happen to the 47 per cent of the Brazilian Amazon that is some kind of protected area.'

But Mr Dill made this sound like an eminently reasonable solution. 'Their goal was to suffocate the producers in the Conservation Units,' he said of the Rousseff government – but that would be bad for the forest. 'The producer ends up not trusting the state and committing environmental crimes and clearing new areas.' Under his proposal, farmers whose properties are regularised would be motivated to maintain their status as good citizens, he said. 'There are more than nineteen million hectares of forest in our region – and we're asking for less than one million hectares to resolve the conflicts.'

Mr Dill frankly conceded that he has received fines on other properties he owns outside the forest. The policy that prevents slaughterhouses from buying animals reared on irregular land such as the forest farm ought to have made the ranch unviable. Mr Dill puffed out his cheeks and described that restriction as little more than an irritation. He raises his cattle to nearly full grown then hands them over to a farmer whose land lies outside the protected area – after which they're sold into the supply chain that promises consumers rainforest-free beef.

Beyond his own ambitions, Mr Dill has big plans for the region – he and other farmers from the area are urging the federal infrastructure programme to move forward on a planned north–south railway to ease congestion on the BR-163 and trying to extend credit to small producers to expand their farms. When the environmental regulations are 'resolved', Novo Progresso will be in a position to flourish, he said. He wished us well on the trip – warning cheerily that, however bad the road had been up until then, it would only get worse from here.

Driving away from the municipal office, we passed a wall painted with neatly

lettered graffiti. 'When the law ignores reality,' it said, 'reality takes revenge on the law.'

6. PLANTING TREES, DRAWING THREATS

The road did indeed steadily deteriorate. We ploughed through banks of loose sand, and at one point found ourselves driving on the wrong side of the highway in a line of trucks that had changed lanes in search of better traction and whose dust obscured our ability to see whether anything was coming directly towards us. In the late afternoon we began to smell smoke again, and soon we were driving past banks of orange fire that roared on both sides of the road. We could feel their heat inside the truck.

The next morning we drove warily into •TRAIRÃO, a town whose name has become synonymous with resource-based conflicts. The source of much of the violence is the trees, which in this region are felled not only to make way for other industries: this is an epicentre of illegal logging. It's a lucrative business – worth an estimated $220 million – and at least half the timber harvested in Brazil is illegal. Logging here isn't clear cutting that leaves open fields; illegal loggers target individual high-value trees, such as a single ipé, forty-five metres tall and nearly two metres around, that will produce $4,000 worth of wood. It might be growing in a conservation area – a national park or forest – or on land owned by the state but not zoned for protection. Or it might be on private land, which under the Forest Code can't legally be logged.

You might think that if a tree or two is taken here or there that doesn't seem like such a big problem. But logging, like mining, has an outsize impact. 'It's deforesting activity that incentivises,' is how Marco Lentini – who has been researching the

business for more than twenty years and currently manages the forest file for the World Wildlife Fund in Brazil – explained it to me. Once loggers open a road they are often followed by hunters, and then by *garimpeiros*, who use the opened track to explore for gold. Then comes the wholesale clearing: the land is set alight, the cheapest and fastest and easiest way to clear the vegetation. 'Logging is the starting point,' Mr Lentini said, 'of colonising the forest.'

It's also deforestation that degrades. The logged patches may appear on those satellite maps as untouched, but biologists have discovered in recent years that the extraction of even a small number of trees has a mammoth impact on biodiversity and the health of the forest. The new openings in the canopy cause it to dry out and be much more susceptible to fires – the majority of which are set deliberately as the last phase of clearing land. There were 89,178 separate fires in the Amazon in 2019.

The loss of the big trees also affects the natural cycles of the lower ones and throws the whole ecosystem out of whack. We are only beginning to understand how damaging this is. New, more sharply focused satellite monitoring shows that from 2007 to 2013 some 102,000 square kilometres of the Amazon were degraded – more than double the area deforested. A study of the biodiversity in degraded forest in Pará found that twice as many species have been lost to degradation as to deforestation.

As with so much else in this country, Brazil has, on paper, a plan to control illegal logging. A licensing system is meant to ensure that timber sold in Brazil or exported is legal – but the system is laughably inefficient, Mr Lentini explained, and easily corrupted. To obtain harvesting

BR-163

CUIABÁ

> "'Once loggers open a road they are often followed by hunters, and then by *garimpeiros*, who use the opened track to explore for gold. Then comes the wholesale clearing.'"

permits landowners bribe officials, or sell illegally harvested trees, claiming they have come from other land they own and are permitted to log, or fudge documents coming out of sawmills. Fake papers are so easy to come by in towns such as Trairão, he said, that he has bought them himself in a matter of minutes.

On the BR-163 we were passing trucks loaded with logs and sawmills with huge tree trunks stacked in the yards. But we weren't finding many people who wanted to talk about logging. In fact, many warned us not even to ask. At the big blue Catholic church in Trairão, which has a well-established programme to help small farmers – who often find themselves in conflict with the loggers – the priests told us we'd be better off leaving town. They had last received death threats from loggers a month before.

But there was one person in Trairão ready to talk about illegal logging: Osvalinda Pereira. She was forty-nine on the day we met, and she projected the peaceful calm of a woman who has lived with danger for so long that nothing much disturbs her any more. Ms Pereira and her husband, Daniel Alves, came to Trairão in 2006. They both grew up poor in the

south and married young, and in the 1990s were given a plot of land in Mato Grosso through INCRA, a government settlement programme. They spent fifteen years there, trying to build up a farm – but a neighbouring soya-plantation owner kept trying to buy them out. (It's illegal but common for people settled through INCRA to sell their land.) Eventually, he took to burning their fruit and nut trees, she says.

When police ignored their complaints they headed further north, thinking they would have more luck in this area where agriculture is still small scale. They found the land near Trairão – INCRA wouldn't resettle them officially, but no one complained when they began to set up a home there. And, instead of clearing trees, they planted more. They began to harvest cacao and cashews, and seeds they sold to reforestation projects. These were ideas she learned from her mother, who raised twelve children on what she gathered in a small patch of forest. 'People said at first that we were crazy,' Ms Pereira said, when she welcomed us into their airy house, nestled in a grove of trees, 'but then they saw what we were doing, and many of them wanted to start doing the same thing.' Ms Pereira set up an association, teaching women in the community how to make a living from the forest. Some of their husbands switched to 'extraction', as it is known, as well.

The logging bosses did not appreciate any of this. They didn't want to compete with her for manual labour, and they didn't like the ethos she was spreading about how the trees had more value left

Pages 124–5: Raimundo, forty-two, has occupied a plot of land close to the Samuel hydroelectric power plant. He needs to cut down the forest to feed the cattle he raises and accuses the government of ignoring the problems faced by the Amazon region.

alive. Neither did they like all this talk of living self-sufficiently from the forest. When the environmental police made a major raid on the loggers in the area in 2013 and burned the logging equipment, the owners blamed her for tipping off the authorities – she says she did nothing of the kind, that she had, rather, been hoping to win people over gradually.

But the reprisals came almost immediately. A woman warned her that four local loggers' associations had put up $1,500 each to pay for a hit man to kill her and her family. A short time later, on a rainy evening, several trucks pulled up in front of their house, and twelve men draped in guns and ammunition appeared at the door. Knowing the neighbours were too far away to hear her scream, Ms Pereira recalls with a wry smile that she and Mr Alves instead invited them in; she made them juice from the fruit she'd harvested.

The loggers said they were there to make a 'deal'. She said she wasn't interested. The leader told her, 'Look, if one of my workers loses his livelihood because of you and they come here and do something to you or your husband – don't blame me.'

'Is that a death threat?' Ms Pereira says she asked him.

'I'm just telling you. Poor people like you only make money when they die,' he replied.

'So kill me now,' she said, 'because if you don't, I'm going to make a criminal complaint against you all.' It was, she says, resignation rather than bravado. She was convinced that they would, in fact, kill her.

For reasons that still mystify her, they didn't. They put down their juice and drove off into the rain. 'They could have done whatever they wanted – we were alone there, and there was no way out ... They have killed so many people, and no one hears about it. No one has the courage to talk about what happens here. Here there is justice for the rich, my dear, but not for the poor.'

Reporting the threats to the law yielded little – no local police station would open a case against the comparatively wealthy and powerful loggers. Gunmen continued to pull up and circle her house periodically on motorbikes. And although federal police finally got involved, the best they had to suggest was that the family move away. They refused. A sort of uneasy detente developed. They abandoned the effort to win others over to extractivism, but they stayed put.

'If we leave, we'll lose what we built here, and they'll keep killing people and nothing will change,' said Ms Pereira 'We already ran from Mato Grosso, and we're not going to run again.' Ms Pereira sees the dense forests that remain in Pará as a sort of last stand for the country. 'We don't want what happened everywhere else in Brazil to happen here.'

Their small farm, an oasis in the forest, where the chickens fussed at our feet and flowered vines crept over the house, presented a weird contrast to the dark story Ms Pereira told. A fierce rainstorm blew in before dusk, and she urged us to get back on the road, not to linger. Mr Alves sketched out a shortcut back to the BR-163 – a road built by loggers to get their loads to the highway more quickly – and we headed off.

We hadn't gone far when the rain cleared, and Aaron wanted to stop to take photos of smouldering, newly cleared land. We pulled the car over and opened the doors. From both sides of the road the forest rang with the buzz of chainsaws.

7. A PEOPLE'S FIGHT FOR SURVIVAL

That night we drove north on the BR-163 to the town of • MIRITITUBA and then left the highway again, this time to board a clunky ferry that took us across the Tapajós River.

In Itaituba, a city of one hundred thousand, we checked into a hotel – it could charitably be called 'modest' – where rooms were running at more than $175 a night. In the morning, when I saw the breakfast room full of men in the uniforms of construction companies and hydro-electric plants, I understood the hefty rates: Itaituba is a boomtown in the making.

By now, ten days into the trip, my shoulders ached from yanking the steering wheel around the giant potholes, my eyes stung from the smoke and the whole world felt like it was coated in a palette of unremitting greys and browns. So when we picked up Alessandra Korap at her house in a small indigenous community on the edge of town in the early morning, and parrots congregated noisily in the mango tree above her house, it already felt like a respite.

She directed us out of the town and on to the Transamazônica, the east–west highway. We drove west for an hour inside the Amazon National Park before turning on to a dirt road leading down to the banks of the Tapajós. A line of boats in varying states of disrepair littered the shore; Ms Korap told us they belonged to *garimpeiros* who use them to dredge the river bottom and travel to access points for sites inside the forest.

Before long there was the growl of a motor, and a teenager from Ms Korap's community piloted a simple outboard to the shore. He lugged aboard the fuel we had brought, piled us in and swept the

boat back out into the rapids that churn along the deep green of the Tapajós. After an hour of racing past unbroken lines of trees, he cut the motor and we came to a stop below a sign, written in Portuguese and Munduruku, that both warned and welcomed us to their land.

The constitution adopted in Brazil in 1988, following the end of the dictatorship, guaranteed the rights of indigenous people to their land, and in the 1990s the government began the process of identifying traditional indigenous territories and handing them over to limited forms of self-government. There is archaeological evidence that the Munduruku have occupied the region of the upper Tapajós for hundreds of years. In the late 1990s they began the process of trying to have the land demarcated, as the process of official recognition is called in Brazil, and they fell into a bureaucratic nightmare that dragged on for more than a decade.

Finally, in the last hours of Ms Rousseff's administration, some 173,000 hectares were provisionally identified for demarcation. But when Mr Temer took over he froze the process again, and Mr Bolsonaro has vowed that not a single centimetre of indigenous land will be demarcated while he is in office. In 2014 the Munduruku did the physical part of the process themselves – cutting a border around their territory through the jungle. That didn't, however, give them legal rights to the land. And that matters. Officially

Pages 132–3: The inhabitants of the Jacundá National Forest accuse the Brazilian federal government of ignoring the population's problems and say they are forced to deforest the area in order to survive.

BR-163

CUIABÁ

designating the land as indigenous would threaten one of the most ambitious infrastructure projects in Brazil.

The *hidrovia* is a plan for forty-nine separate dams on the Tapajós and its tributaries, meant to quell the rapids and create a 2,200-kilometre stretch of placid water on which grains could be moved north to the Amazon River on barges that hold 50,000 tonnes compared to forty-tonne trucks. Among the investors in the project is China's Three Gorges Development Corporation. When operational, the dams would generate twenty-nine gigawatts of electricity, equal to 25 per cent of Brazil's current usage. The biggest of the dams would be more than seven kilometres across and require clearing nearly a million hectares of forest. The Munduruku territory would be obliterated.

The Munduruku have been fighting the dams for eight years now – in a canny campaign that they focused not on Brasilia as much as on Europe, where the citizens of countries sympathetic to indigenous people might put pressure on Brazil. They have managed to have the building of the first two stages suspended while the Supreme Court considers whether their claim to the land is enough to stop the project. But until they have demarcation they cannot claim indigenous land, and in the hotel lobby in Itaituba, as men in suits and men in industrial overalls bustled past me in all directions, the prospects for such official recognition seemed remote indeed.

Our young boat pilot nosed us into an opening in the trees, and Ms Korap led us ashore and along a short jungle path to a clearing. There we found Juarez Saw, the *cacique*, or chief, working with his family. They had just brought in a harvest of manioc, and three generations were engaged in mashing it, draining the cyanide that occurs in it naturally, shredding

and roasting it in a vast metal pan to make flour. The *cacique* welcomed us graciously and sat us down to explain why the Munduruku won't get their right to their land recognised in today's Brazil.

'We used to think it was the dams that were the issue. Today we see that the dams are just the foot in the door,' he said. 'After they build the dams, other projects come after it, projects to export soya, mines, ranches, sawmills.' Already Munduruku land is peppered with *garimpo* mines. 'But we know the *garimpos*, the little guys, they won't stay. It's the big foreign mines who are going to get control of this region.'

Just the day before, Mr Saw told us, he and some of his family had been out hunting in the forest when they heard illegal loggers at work on the indigenous land. They left the loggers to it. 'We can't do anything. We've been repeatedly threatened by them. If we want to survive any longer we have to keep quiet. We can only report them to ICMBio for them to enforce the law – but they aren't able to do it.'

It would not be difficult, in his village, to romanticise the role of Brazil's indigenous people in protecting the forest – to see their way of life as holding some sort of key to human survival. On the day we spent in • SAWRÉ-MUYBU, Mr Saw and his family moved easily through the tangled trees and vines, racing across slim branches balanced over swamps, moving swiftly up and down the hills at the riverbank. In late afternoon children lined up to plunge one after the other into an ice-cold stream.

Yet, as Chief Juarez himself observed, there are Munduruku working in the *garimpo* on their land and Munduruku who do illegal logging. They do it, he said, for money. He does not want his people to live entirely isolated in the forest: they need better health care, and better education,

BR-163

CUIABÁ

and options for young people. But the change must be on their terms, he said – and those are terms that settler Brazil does not seem to grasp.

We left Sawré-Muybu just in time for our pilot to navigate the rapids before dark, and in the morning we caught the ferry back to Miritituba.

8. 'MILLIONS OF ANTHILLS IN THE FOREST'

On the BR-163 once again, we faced our last – and longest – drive through what, on paper, was hundreds of kilometres of protected forest. Instead, again, we found farms and fire. By now that came as no surprise. We drove for eleven hours, and the sun was about to set once more when we reached the last stretch of the BR-163, which threads into the city of ● SANTARÉM. The road ends at the gate of a huge installation built on the riverbank by the Minnesota-based food conglomerate Cargill.

Santarém's port buildings are a bulky, modern contrast to the low, gentle sprawl of the rest of this city, where, nearly five hundred years ago, Jesuit missionaries began to build a town on the site of a settlement of Tapajós indigenous people. Today Santarém has an economy growing at three times the national average, and its population is expected to hit 600,000 next year.

In the morning we went to see Higo de Sousa – a deputy to the state's top environmental official, whose office is 1,500 kilometres away in the capital, Belém. He enquired about our journey, and when we told him of the smoke and the craters on the BR-163 he just laughed.

'You can't imagine what a paradise it is now. It used to take us a month to get to Novo Progresso,' he said about a journey that now can be made in two long days.

Mr Sousa was eager to describe the many ways the state is attempting to control illegal activity in the forest. In the same way that slaughterhouses have to say where they get their cattle and Cargill has to buy soya from producers that have registered their land, the government wants to make gold buyers verify their sources of ore, he said.

But the longer we talked, the more Mr Sousa's outward optimism seemed to fade. I told him about how the cattle ranchers we met described the way they circumvent the system. Timber buyers, he acknowledged with a sigh, do the same. 'That's our life – we set up a process, they find a way around it. There are 853 known *garimpo* sites around Itaituba alone, he added. 'You can't stop it – there are millions of these anthills in the forest – by the time you get there they're hiding in the woods.' Not long ago he travelled two days by road and boat with a two-person police escort to inspect a huge plantation being carved into the forest illegally. When he got there he was confronted by an armed militia. 'So we turned around and travelled two days home again.'

By the time we had been talking for a couple of hours Mr Sousa had boiled the situation down to a question of power. 'The big agricultural producers, the ones with the most capital, are the ones at the front of politics here,' he said, and they are the ones who will determine what happens to the forest. 'When you see it from the outside it doesn't look so complex. When I started in this job, I thought, "OK, let's fight the loggers, the miners, the ranchers" – but when I got a good look at it, I was just a small dot in the giant canvas.'

Mr Sousa concluded, half joking, 'The planet is depending on me.' Then he buried his face in his hands. 'For the love of God ...'

BR-163

THE INDIGENOUS CHAMPIONSHIP

Even great stars like Neymar began by taking part in *peladas*, games played on little neighbourhood pitches in unofficial tournaments. Brazil's largest *pelada* takes place in Manaus, the capital of Amazonas state, and the neighbouring small towns. It has been running since 1973 and can involve up to a thousand teams with as many as twenty-three thousand players, hence its name, Peladão, the 'big *pelada*'. It is played barefoot on bare-earth pitches. For the past few years the Peladão has included games restricted to teams made up of native Brazilians, the Peladão Indígena, with fourteen clubs and around 230 players from groups such as the Tikunas, the Karapanã or the Sateré-Mawé. Some teams competing in the

Peladão are composed of players from a single community, whereas others bring together twenty-seven ethnicities speaking fourteen different languages (although they seem to understand each other well enough on the pitch).

Or there are teams composed of a single ethnicity but with members who come from far-flung areas, from villages and towns many kilometres apart from each other. The Peladão Indígena was created as a means of promoting social relations, and, in line with developments in official football, it has launched a section open to women's teams, which for the players (often *ribeirinhas*, women from riverside communities) represents an assertion of independence and their fight against the prevailing prejudices in their own communities.

9. THE ROAD THAT LIES AHEAD

Before I started on this trip I knew a couple of things. I knew that deforestation rates were climbing again. I knew that forest degradation was happening as fast or faster than clear cutting and that far less attention was being paid to it. I also knew that there was good news in this story: the Amazon has some degree of resilience. Up to 25 per cent of the forest that has ever been cleared has grown back. That represents a new source of stored carbon for the world and holds the promise of restored biodiversity. I also knew that some of the measures that would make a real difference to preserving the Amazon are relatively straightforward. That regrown forest, for example, could be monitored. The satellites that sweep over the Amazon take no pictures of regrowth: once a patch of forest is marked as cleared it is subsequently skipped in the tracking. Something as simple as turning a camera on it now would enable the government to monitor what is regrowing.

Brazilian agriculture is hugely inefficient, something I'd been reading on paper for years but understood in a new way when I drove through the endless fields of newly cleared pasture right next to previously cleared land that had been abandoned. Brazil does need a stronger agricultural sector; it is a vital part of the economy, just as Mr Ferrarin and the other farmers insisted. But Brazil doesn't need to clear a single additional hectare to make farming vastly more productive. In the Amazon alone there are ten million hectares of abandoned or poorly used pastures: an area the size of Iceland, wasted.

Pages 136–7: Illegal deforestation in the Jacundá National Forest.

With technical assistance to farmers and ranchers – teaching them about crop rotation to prevent pasture degradation, for example, and using water tanks instead of ponds for cattle – the sector could expand without losing another hectare of forest. At the same time, by stripping corruption and bureaucratic inefficiency out of its land-titling system, Brazil could deliver ownership documents to Brazilians who are already legally farming in the Amazon, turning their farms into collateral for credit that they could then reinvest to increase their productivity. And the government could stop settling poor farmers in the forest – people with no assets and no technical support who have little choice but to clear land for cattle because they have no other way to make a living.

For the more than half of farming that is already made possible by government credit, such credit could be conditional on farmers demonstrating compliance with the Forest Code. And government spending – on credit but also on infrastructure such as roads and bridges – could be prioritised for municipalities that are operating within the Code: the likes of Vice-Mayor Gelson Dill's Novo Progresso could be blacklisted until a majority of properties are compliant. In addition, the research institute Imazon found that a quarter of all deforestation in the Amazon in 2016 took place on public land that hadn't been zoned. As a result, no one is assigned to monitor what happens on that land. By converting it into Conservation Units and recognised indigenous territory the government could dampen the market in land speculation.

Logging, ironically, could also be a way to protect the forest. Marco Lentini of the World Wildlife Fund described as 'reasonably well managed' the 2.5 million hectares of Amazon that are currently licensed and

'In the Amazon there are ten million hectares of abandoned or poorly used pastures: an area the size of Iceland, wasted.'

used for sustainable logging (four or five of the oldest trees per hectare are removed each year). Those swathes of forest are safe and monitored. But there is so much consumer concern now about dirty supply chains and about rainforest wood in general that people don't want to buy even from such legal producers, he said, adding, 'I think we need to use the forest to give it value.'

These steps are not easy, but they are manageable in the context of what Brazil has been able to do already. But what I understood only once I'd driven the road was how intense are the pressures to do something different.

The thirty million people who live in the forest want better lives, and so do millions more Brazilians. It does not follow that these can only be achieved by blindly harvesting the trees, digging out the minerals, damming the rivers, clearing the forest for pastures. There is, in fact, compelling data to show that all these resources would ultimately be worth more left in place. But those who hold power in Brazil today – and who are signing deals and making decisions about irrevocable steps in the Amazon – don't see it that way. They see a resource whose value is to be maximised immediately. They have willing partners, in China in particular, ready to fund the infrastructure that guarantees a steady flow of food, and in companies such as Cargill, ready to process it in the supply chain of their giant transnational businesses.

Almost everyone I met on our journey talked about the price they were being asked to pay – to protect the forest or to develop it. The ranchers and the farmers asked why the cost of stored carbon and recycled rain should come out of their pockets. The Munduruku wonder why their survival must be bartered for a growing economy that will fund Brazil's pensions and universities. Should Western consumers bear some of the cost, too, by paying more for sustainable rainforest products, for wooden decks or soya-based pet food or steak? Everything – wood, soya, cattle – raised on farms compliant with the Forest Code costs more because it comes from a reduced area of productive land on property that's mostly forest. And auditing those supply chains costs money, too.

One day not long after our trip I sat in my office in Rio and clicked open the latest satellite feed of images of the Amazon. I thought about how silent and how clean it looked from above, with wisps of cloud across the images – and also, once you know what you're looking at, how crowded. And I remembered Mila Ferreira, the environmental protection agent, and something she told me when we were standing in a smouldering field with bemused cows watching us eat a pineapple we were given by a friendly, unhelpful farmer.

'For me, the best days are when we fly over the forest,' she said, 'because down here we're just in the middle of destruction – but when you're up there you see things on a different scale. That, despite all the damage, there is still a lot of forest. And it's beautiful to see that it's still there.' ✒

Real Life on the Passarela do Samba

After decades of toeing the line,
samba schools are now engaging
with the socio-political issues at
the heart of the contemporary debate.

AYDANO ANDRÉ MOTTA
Translated by Laura Garmeson

Left: Decorative detail from
the allegorical float used
by the Mancha Verde samba
school in São Paolo.

The great samba schools of Rio de Janeiro navigated the 20th century and entered the 21st grappling with a conceptual paradox: they had long tried to appeal to the Brazilian elite only to be systematically rejected. Since the first carnival parade in 1932 and over the decades that followed they fought for acceptance and struggled to gain the approval of those in power, but they remained marginalised and have survived to the present day without ever being afforded the true level of recognition that they deserve, given that they stage one of the most important cultural events not just in Brazil but anywhere in the world: the Rio Carnival. They have always been at best tolerated by an intolerant society, a society that dreams of being different but is ashamed of its own charms. It is only recently that the major players of the Rio Carnival – having been left to fend for themselves, stifled by a lack of funding and the destructive fury of religious fanaticism – have started to develop a more oppositional political identity, bringing the playful spectacle into closer contact with the harsh realities of life. But there is still a long road ahead.

Samba and its various schools have been scarred by the deep-rooted racism in Brazilian society, which has a profound impact on all relations in the country. A product of the African diaspora, carnival and its music pay the high price of this discrimination, but carnival's energy and exuberance – like the Afro-Brazilian population itself – has made Rio de Janeiro the unique place it is today.

In 2019 this quintessentially carioca art form was used to comment, as part of the Mangueira samba school's show, on the unjust and unequal foundations of Brazilian society. Their song 'História para Ninar Gente Grande' ('A Bedtime Story for Grown-Ups') celebrated 'the country that's not in the portrait' and shone a light on events and figures that have been erased by the official white-colonial narrative. The samba lyric, voted the best that year, included the line 'since 1500 there have been more invasions than discoveries', a reference to the modern reading of the arrival of Pedro Álvares Cabral, the European who 'discovered' Brazil, in a land that had an indigenous population. If humans were there already then there was nothing for the Portuguese navigator to discover; in reality, he invaded. The audience at the Passarela do Samba (Rio's Sambadrome) was visibly moved while watching the school pay tribute to Marielle Franco, the city councillor murdered in Rio in March 2018 and whose death was mourned around the world. Acclaimed by the public, Mangueira were crowned the winners of carnival that year, at a time in their eighty-year odyssey when the

AYDANO ANDRÉ MOTTA is a journalist who writes for the *Jornal do Brasil*, *O Dia* and *O Globo* as well as working as a commentator for the channel SporTV. His research into the Rio carnival has featured in two books, *Maravilhosa e Soberana – Histórias da Beija-Flor* and *Onze Mulheres Incríveis do Carnaval Carioca* (both Verso Brasil Editora, 2012, 2013), that were published in a series of books on samba.

samba schools were at their most critical of society.

A couple of decades ago the key players in the show at the Sambadrome on the Avenida Marquês de Sapucaí were under siege by any number of enemies – economic, political and religious. The latter two joined forces as a wave of conservative faith swept through the country preaching regressive practices and attacking carnival with all their might. At the centre of this battle was a dispute over worshippers. Neo-Pentecostal churches proliferated in poor neighbourhoods, attracting local residents with prosperity theology, a religious doctrine based on non-traditional interpretations of the Bible, which argues that financial rewards in this life are God's will for Christians. According to this doctrine, worshippers can increase their material wealth through faith, positive thinking and donations to Christian ministers (for more on this, see 'Prosperity Now' on page 79).

The *favelas*, poor neighbourhoods and peripheral cities are traditionally home to followers of *Umbanda* and *Candomblé*, religions of African origin brought to Brazil by descendants of the black diaspora. Faith and samba were historically linked – that is, until the neo-Pentecostal rift. Conversion required renouncing the rhythm of the *batucada*, the samba percussive style, which the Catholics, too, regard as profane. This led samba schools to lose members, especially from the *baianas* – the women who wear the traditional dress of those who hosted the early samba *rodas* in the second half of the 19th century – and the percussionists

known as *ritmistas*. Even as early as the 1990s some schools were forced to look for new members to bolster the numbers in these two groups.

The power of the neo-Pentecostal pastors reached the polls, first in parliament and then when they triumphed in Rio's mayoral elections in 2016. The current mayor, Marcelo Crivella, a bishop of the Universal Church of the Kingdom of God (who is also the nephew of the leader of the church, Edir Macedo), even had the support of samba school leaders, a strategic error for which the *sambistas* would pay dearly. As part of the project to stamp out anything related to the Afro-Brazilian religions, the mayor tried to sabotage the parade, withdrawing municipal subsidies to starve the schools of funding and so making it difficult for them to survive throughout the year.

Money was already tight, as sponsorship deals had started to dry up in 2010 for several reasons. The samba schools, whose leaders were often involved in running the *Jogo do Bicho*, or Animal Game – a gambling lottery that had started in Rio under the Portuguese Empire to support the city's zoo but which was outlawed in the 1940s and forced underground where it continues to flourish – began to attract a bad reputation as a result, thus alienating companies who feared exposure to the risks of non-compliance. The corporate image suffered significant damage through its ties with a sector that persistently failed to adopt good management practices. Against this murky backdrop, municipalities, state governors and foreign countries, prompted by the push

This page and page 147: Workers at the Mancha Verde samba school prepare props for the 2020 São Paolo carnival.

THE PASSENGER   Aydano André Motta

for greater financial transparency, followed suit. This put an end to the samba themes that celebrated various locations – from Manaus to Switzerland, Brasilia to Equatorial Guinea, Ceará to Venezuela – which had previously thrown money at the festival in return for publicity at the ultimate good-time showcase.

On top of that, the LIESA (the Independent League of Samba Schools) and Rio's prefecture have been pushing a misguided image of the parade and the activities of its samba schools, insisting on making carnival about business rather than culture. In their attempts to attract foreign tourists they have turned their backs on locals and Brazilian visitors, failing to appreciate that the schools are primarily about culture, community life, belonging to and celebrating the Afro-Brazilian population. In disregarding these values they do the show and the city a great disservice.

Then came the decline, after a long period of coexistence with power. The LIESA, created in 1985 to oversee the event and organise the show, entered into a partnership with Globo, Brazil's largest media group, and established sponsorship deals with, among others, Bradesco (one of the country's biggest private banks) and Coca-Cola. The carnival directors – not the *sambistas* – started to host politicians and business executives on their floats on the Avenida da Samba.

Over the past fifteen years or so Rio has seen the rise of the *blocos de rua*, the street bands that are now the most important part of carnival. Some of them, like Cordão da Bola Preta, founded in 1918, attract more than a million people to the city centre on the Saturday morning of the festival. Simpatia É Quase Amor has on average 400,000 people attending their show, which takes place on Ipanema beach. Rio has approximately 450 *blocos* of all different sizes, styles and audiences. Diversity, tolerance and variety, free of charge, on the street – an irresistible combination.

The samba schools, exiled in their ghettos and facing the prospect of dwindling resources, with the elite turning their backs yet again, have at last started to display a degree of critical awareness. After more than eighty parades they're finally adopting more controversial themes – with the 2018 display proving to be the most political carnival to date, featuring critical positions from four out of the thirteen schools parading through the Sambadrome.

'My God, My God, Is Slavery Extinct?' was the *enredo* (the main samba theme) of samba school Paraíso do Tuiuti, developed by the *carnavalesco* Jack Vasconcelos. The school sang about racism, attacked the labour reforms approved by Congress and featured the figure of a vampire wearing a presidential sash in their final allegorical float, a portrayal of the president of the day, Michel Temer, who came to power following the parliamentary coup against the elected Dilma Rousseff in 2016.

The Mangueira samba school, headed by *carnavalesco* Leandro Vieira – who is currently the most important artist at the festival – targeted Rio's mayor with their theme 'Money or No Money, I'm Having a Good Time', which referenced the fact that carnival is a festival of the poor, that happiness doesn't cost a thing and that the bishop wouldn't be able to put a dampener on the festivities.

Beija-Flor highlighted corruption, poverty and violence with their theme 'The True Monster Is the One Who Doesn't Know How to Love: Children Abandoned by the Country that Made Them'. In an excellent samba they channelled various Brazilian frustrations with the conservative narrative – which proved victorious

'"The city, created to expel the French, decided one day that it would reinvent itself as French, in denial of the fact that it was black and indigenous."'

in the presidential elections the following October – and which, against the odds, won them the title.

For 2020 the approach was the same. Once again Mangueira attacked religious conservatism, presenting a black Jesus from the *favela* in 'The Truth Will Set You Free'. Acadêmicos do Grande Rio called for religious tolerance in 'Tata Londirá: The Song of the Caboclo in Caxias Quilombo', about Joãozinho da Gomeia, a *Candomblé* priest. Mocidade Independente addressed the struggle for women's empowerment and gender violence in 'Elza Deusa Soares', a tribute to the legendary samba singer Elza Soares.

As Brazilian historian Luiz Antônio Simas observes, from their very beginnings the samba schools and the popular festival have always existed in the cracks, flirting with transgression and trying to get the attention of those in power. 'The *sambista* should always present himself wearing a linen suit and panama hat,' declared Paulo Benjamin de Oliveira, otherwise known as Paulo da Portela (1901–49), the founding artist who came up with the samba school format. He created the parade procession, the most natural formation for the samba rhythm. The energetic, percussion-led musical style takes hold of people's bodies and transforms them, resulting in the swaying walk, the beautiful and sensual on-the-spot dance. It should be practised, he instructed, with impeccable elegance to dispel any prejudice.

Brazil having been the world's principal destination for African slaves for many centuries (particularly between 1758 and 1831), Rio has reflected Brazilian racism like no other city. Freed slaves were left to fend for themselves with no social support whatsoever, forced to settle in the surrounding hills – forming the *favelas*, home to an abundance of cultural riches and deep social deprivation – and the North Zone, while the Centre and South Zones nurtured dreams that were never realised of becoming a 'Tropical Paris'. 'The city, created to expel the French, who were trying to invade Brazil, decided one day that it would reinvent itself as French, in denial of the fact that it was black and indigenous,' explains Simas.

The coastal metropolis, encircled by mountains swathed in the Atlantic Forest, grew according to the perverse logic of violence, but its creative and charming inhabitants were sunny and musical, lovers of a simple coexistence in the streets. All these characteristics are present in the samba parades, which spread throughout the suburbs, forced always to contend with the hostility of those in power.

These lyrics are taken from the first recorded samba: 'The chief of police calls me on the telephone to say / That in the Carioca there's a roulette I can play'. Composed in 1917, 'Pelo Telefone' ('On the Telephone'), by Donga and Mauro de Almeida, is a song about the tolerant behaviour of the police in the face of the population's transgressive recreational habits and predilection for flirting with the forbidden. As part of its European 'whitening' project, the Rio elite (and the Brazilian elite in general) looked down on anything associated with the Afro-Brazilian community. When in doubt they banned practices like samba as part of a

widespread project of subjugation. The 'exotic' rhythms, which could be traced back to the drumming of slaves who would gather to allay their nostalgia for Africa, were – in the white racist view – repulsive, indecent and profane, which led to the *sambistas* being persecuted by the police.

Samba artists would meet at the houses of such pioneers as Hilária Batista de Almeida, known as Tia Ciata (1854–1924), a cook and *baiana* priestess who hosted the first samba *rodas* in Praça Onze, a neighbourhood on the edge of the city centre, during the second half of the 19th century. The distrustful tolerance of the lawmakers meant that samba schools were eventually accepted in their communities, and Paulo da Portela established the elegant dress code of linen suit and panama hat, which gave the activity an air of 'decency and civility' (from a white perspective). It was an aesthetic nod and a bid for acceptance.

How the school that bears his name came to be called Portela is a testament to the logic of repression. Each year the directors of Vai Como Pode (the original name of the school) were required to secure a permit from the police to parade. In a surreal episode of Brazilian bureaucracy, during their 1936 visit to the police station to renew their licence to take part in the festivities something went wrong – the police chief, Dulcídio Gonçalves, considered Vai Como Pode to be a 'vulgar' name and denied them permission. This led to a stand-off, followed by heated discussion, until the authorities asked where the parade would be taking place. 'On the Estrada do Portela,' they replied. 'That settles it then. The name will be Portela.' And the sound of the stamp validating the document sealed the deal and formalised the baptism – at the police station – of the most important samba school of them all.

The school that was to become Portela's main rival arrived on the scene not long after Portela was founded. Mangueira, a *favela* on the edge of the North Zone, had grown up following the slum clearances of the early 20th century – overseen by the mayor, Pereira Passos, the man who sought to reinvent Rio as a 'Tropical Paris' – when residents from the city centre, ex-slaves and low-skilled workers, the vast majority of whom were black, were moved out of their homes and forced up the hillsides to find a place to live. Many *sambistas* who had trained at the *rodas* in Praça Onze were among them, and the school they founded was to become the most important carnival group to originate in a *favela*. *Blocos* soon emerged and transformed the *favela* into a little haven of happiness with each carnival. On 28 April 1928 eight participants from these groups decided to set up a samba school – the Estação Primeira de Mangueira (the First Station of Mangueira). Angenor de Oliveira, known as Cartola, leader of the movement and one of the greatest samba artists of all time, chose the colours – green and pink – and the name, in reference to the railway line that ran through the area. To this day Mangueira is still the first stop after the Central do Brasil station (the main point of departure for train lines in the city centre) where a samba school can be found.

Almost four years later the schools began to discover their competitive nature, participating in the same parade in Tia Ciata's Praça Onze. The first show in 1932 was promoted by the newspaper *Mundo Sportivo* and featured just five schools. The following year another daily, *O Globo*, funded the parade, and this one had twenty-five participants. Five more joined in 1934, organised by a third newspaper, *A Hora*. This energy combined with

> 'Carnival has cemented the image Rio in the eyes of the world as the happiness capital, democratic, inclusive and egalitarian, without repression or restraint.'

deep African roots to unite Rio's black community in their religious celebrations and in the samba *rodas*. More major schools emerged – Império Serrano, Vila Isabel, União da Ilha do Governador, Beija-Flor de Nilópolis, Unidos do Viradouro, Acadêmicos do Salgueiro and Mocidade Independente de Padre Miguel among others. Each would, in due course, establish themselves as rivals to the pioneering Portela and Mangueira schools.

Competition is in the samba schools' DNA; they experience carnival as a time of anxiety, rivalry and commitment to the constant pursuit of aesthetic and rhythmic perfection – well beyond joy, revelry and play. No parade is complete without a dispute over the title, fighting over funding and the satisfaction of a mission accomplished. The cliché that it takes all year to prepare for a single street show is nothing less than the absolute truth. This dedication has consolidated the idea of the parade as a spectacle that is carioca in the purest sense and one of the most celebrated aspects of Rio. It has cemented the image of the city in the eyes of the world as the happiness capital, democratic, inclusive and egalitarian, without repression or restraint.

Each presentation has a theme that changes every year and determines the production of the fantasies and allegories as well as the composition of the *samba-enredo* (the unique samba based on the theme) itself. Despite playing such a significant role, it took some time for the schools to grasp how powerful these themes could be. Up to the late 1950s they adhered to the official white-colonial narrative in their attempt to win over the elite, and it wasn't until a child of the middle classes discovered the display that they became aware of the urgent need to change their approach.

Fernando Pamplona, a scenographer at the Municipal Theatre, joined the parade in 1959 as a member of the jury and fell in love with the Salgueiro samba school. The next year he became a *carnavalesco* and suggested the theme 'Quilombo dos Palmares', the name of a colonial-era slave enclave located in the Brazilian Northeast in what is today the state of Alagoas. This theme made history as the first step in a great aesthetic revolution, one that still valued fantasy and allegory but also had an important political significance: black people were taking back control of their own narratives, ancestors and beliefs. Carnival took on a new meaning and began to attract the attention of a section of the rich, who started to show interest in the samba schools.

The 1964 military coup profoundly altered life in Brazil, not least for those involved in carnival. In 1969 Império Serrano, the school from the Madureira district founded by workers at the carioca port, sang in 'Heroes of Freedom': 'Oh, oh, oh / Freedom Lord / Night would pass, day would come / The black man's blood would run / Day by day / Lament to lament / Agony to agony / He called for / The end of tyranny', a masterful theme voicing overt political opposition at the height of the regime.

The political tide suddenly turned within the schools. Embedded in the poorest areas of Rio, they extolled Brazil's

The Mancha Verde samba
school, winner of the 2019
São Paolo carnival, prepares
for the 2020 event.

THE CARNAVAL DE RUA

What takes place in the Sambadrome – the
official competition between the samba
schools admitted to the two evenings of the
big contest – is just a part of Rio's carnival,
although perhaps the most visible. In fact,
the city is besieged for about ten days by
another, fluid, sprawling, all-encompassing
carnival, the Carnaval de Rua, with its
colourful participants, the *blocos de rua*.
For as long as the city's celebrations
have existed, the *blocos* have taken to
the streets. These groups are sometimes
organised, sometimes spontaneous, and
they have helped to define the identity
of the Rio Carnival. Cordão de Bola
Preta, established in 1918, Cacique de
Ramos, dating from the 1960s, and the
Banda de Ipanema, perhaps the greatest

concentration of drag queens you will see anywhere in one place at any one time, are some of the big names in the tradition that still meet and parade through the streets. Over time, alongside the historic *blocos*, dozens of little groups have formed, all with their regulation banner, musical instruments, obligatory masks, wigs and slogans. The following are some of the current favourites, parading perhaps at dawn on the Saturday before Lent or on Ash Wednesday: Simpatia É Quase Amor, Bloco das Carmelitas (because they climb the steep slopes of Santa Teresa beside the Carmelite convent) and, perhaps the most closely followed and colourful of them all, Bloco Céu na Terra. And what do they have in common? Being open to everyone: the *blocos* represent the truly democratic face of carnival.

economic miracle – a period when the nation's GDP began to grow by 14 per cent a year and enthusiasm for the government reached insane levels – and brought a nationalistic fervour to the city streets. Many of them praised aspects of the dictatorship, but the most famous case would mark Beija-Flor for ever. Three of their themes between 1973 and 1975 shamelessly celebrated the dictator. The most famous of these was 'Brasil do Ano 2000' ('Brazil in the Year 2000') from 1974, with lyrics about oil 'flowing from the ground in abundance' and a refrain that ran: 'He who lives shall see / Our land so altered / The order of progress / Will push Brazil onwards'.

The decline of the dictatorship in the 1980s permeated the themes of the parade. In 1984, at the newly inaugurated Passarela do Samba on the Avenida Marquês de Sapucaí, the Em Cima da Hora samba school addressed problems that poorer workers endured on public transport in '33, Destino D. Pedro II' ('33, Destination D. Pedro II'). With lyrics about the 'suburban worker arriving late' and the stratospheric inflation of the time, they cited the impunity of the 'pickpocket who almost always gets away with it' and created the perfect description, a marriage of plain speech and irony, of daily life for this section of the population: 'Let's exalt through poetry / The meaning of our daily routine / To earn a crust / I wake up early in the morning / Walk to the station / To get to D. Pedro / In time to punch my time card / It ain't easy, no / What with inflation / To long for my rights / And the progress of the nation'.

At this time themes critical of the government were almost completely absent from carnival. One notable exception was the following year, when Caprichosos de Pilares guaranteed their place at the Olympics of politically critical themes with '... E por Falar em Saudade' ('... And While We're Talking About Nostalgia'). Under the pretext of a discourse on the past, they raised the subject of the theft of the Jules Rimet cup, the World Cup trophy, in the late 1970s ('The national team / Who melted down the trophy wearing their best poker face') and expressed the national anxiety about democracy ('The people are due to choose the president') just months after the campaign for direct elections was defeated in Congress.

On the Passarela, Brazil's political agenda didn't make much of an appearance, however – samba schools preferred to court the sponsorship of corporations and governments through escapist themes. There were exceptions, as in 1988 when the centenary of the abolition of slavery was practically the only theme. Mangueira stepped up to the plate again with '100 Anos de Liberdade, Realidade ou Ilusão?' ('100 Years of Freedom, Reality or Illusion?'): 'Perhaps ... / The Golden Law we dreamed about / Signed so long ago / Was not really the end of slavery / Today, in reality / Where is freedom / Where nobody saw it / Young man / Don't you forget that the black man built / The riches of our Brazil / Ask the Creator / Who painted this picture / Free from the whip of the cotton-picker / Trapped in the poverty of the *favela*'.

In 1996 Império Serrano gambled on a social theme that paid tribute to the sociologist Herbert de Sousa, known as Betinho, and his campaign against hunger (the country was plunging, as it so often has, into extreme social inequality). The theme was 'Thou Wilt See that a Son of Thine Flees Not from Battle', a line from the Brazilian national anthem, and the song spoke of the urgent need for change, of agricultural reform and the problem of urban violence: 'I want to have my land / My patch of earth, my share / It's no secret

Carnival means samba, but samba does not necessarily mean carnival. Many of the great *sambistas* are certainly linked to the festival, if only because it is not just an event but also a state of mind, a feeling of freedom – and yet some of the composers of carnival samba have also extended their influence far from the celebrations. Take Paulinho da Viola. One of his most famous sambas, 'Foi um Rio que Passou em Minha Vida', is dedicated to the Portela samba school, which has its roots in the Rio suburb of Madureira. In popular culture Viola is identified with the school's blue-and-white colours, but his output has had an impact far beyond the street party. The same goes for Angenor de Oliveira, known as Cartola, who lived for many years in the *favela* of Mangueira, home to the school of the same name and to which he dedicated some beautiful compositions; but his work goes beyond that and includes some of Brazil's best-loved songs, including 'As Rosas Não Falam' and 'Amor Proibido'. Like his, the hearts of other key figures in classic samba belonged to Mangueira, including Nelson Cavaquinho and Carlos Cachaça, whereas Zé Keti had ties with Portela. But it would be a mistake to think that traditional samba, *samba de raiz*, is confined exclusively to the past. You only need think of a composer like Moacyr Luz, who, as well as being responsible for a huge (and wonderful) songbook, is also the central figure in another party, the Samba do Trabalhador, a long-running musical gathering that takes place every Monday in the garden of the Club Renascença, a lively social club in the Andaraí neighbourhood far removed from the city centre.

that / The poor man is hungry / The rich man is afraid'.

Beija-Flor adopted a similar tone in 2003 (the year they won) to celebrate the election of Luiz Inácio Lula da Silva as president the previous year. Under the theme 'The People Will Tell Their Own Story: An Empty Bag Can't Stand Upright, the Hand that Starts a War Can Make Peace', the refrain from the Nilópolis district's anthem meant they could issue a warning that sounded like a threat: 'I want freedom, dignity and unity / I was made of tin, now I am silver / Trash, gold from the region / Tired of earning so little / I'm suffocating, I've got to get it off my chest / Stop this greed then the suffering / Can end'. This, we should note, was the same samba school that, thirty carnivals earlier, had celebrated the military dictatorship.

Now things are finally changing, and real Brazilian life, with all its flaws and contradictions, will increasingly find its place on the Passarela do Samba.

The War

A ten-year-old boy
belonging to a group
of drug traffickers
affiliated to the PCC
fires a gun.

Two factions are vying for control of the drug market, the prisons and the *favelas* in an all-out battle for supremacy throughout Brazil.

**BRUNO PAES MANSO
AND CAMILA NUNES DIAS**
Translated by Laura Garmeson

I n a private room in a prison in Mato Grosso do Sul, after a great deal of persistence and negotiation with the local authorities, a prisoner agrees to be interviewed for a research study. Making little attempt to hide the tension in his eyes, which are screwed tight with rage, Carlos walks into the room at the facility. Wearing no handcuffs or prison uniform, he looks to be a little over thirty, has light-brown skin, a thin nose and lips and a stocky physique that commands respect. Sitting down in the chair he looks as if he's about to break the silence in a place where the less you say the more your words are worth. There seems to be something bothering him that he's determined to get off his chest. When he opens his mouth he is clearly missing two front teeth.

'Go on then, spit it out. What do you want to know?' Carlos taunts. 'You want to know about the war between the gangs, right?' Of course, there was no denying it. That was the main reason for arranging this meeting in December 2016. The Brazilian penal system was experiencing a period of uncertainty. The most powerful criminal gang in Brazil, the Primeiro Comando da Capital (PCC), had broken the non-aggression pact it had maintained since its formation with the Comando Vermelho (CV), a criminal group that originated in Rio de Janeiro and had branches across other states.

At the time it was hard to know how to view this conflict. Things would only become clearer a few weeks later – specifically from 1 January 2017 – when a spate of prison riots resulting in the deaths of more than 160 inmates sent shockwaves throughout Brazil. The fuse had been lit the previous June when a note was copied out and passed around in prisons and via WhatsApp. It was an internal message – known as a *salve* – from the PCC, announcing it was breaking with the CV. Isolated conflicts broke out over the second half of that year. Hurt and resentment were simmering until they erupted in an explosion on New Year's Eve. One of the first signs of the crisis that would play out within the prison system was the assault on Carlos four months earlier.

'You see my teeth?' he asks, pointing to the gaping holes in the upper part of his mouth. 'They were broken. I was the first person to be attacked by the PCC here in Mato Grosso do Sul.' Carlos was one of the leaders of the Comando Vermelho in the neighbouring state of Mato Grosso, where the group is

CAMILA NUNES DIAS is a sociologist and professor at the Federal University of ABC, Brazil. She studies Brazilian gangs and is one of the few people outside the criminal networks to be in contact with their leaders and to have access to documentation of their activities.

BRUNO PAES MANSO is a journalist and researcher for São Paulo University's Centre for the Study of Violence. His articles on crime have been published in magazines and newspapers such as *Piauí* and *Folha de S. Paulo*. He is the author of *Homicide in São Paulo: An Examination of Trends from 1960–2010* (Springer, 2016) and *A Guerra: A Ascensão do PCC e o Mundo do Crime no Brasil*, written with Camila Nunes Dias, from which this piece is taken.

referred to as the CV-MT. He was serving a sentence in Campo Grande because in April that year he had been caught in possession of drugs in a small city on the outskirts of the capital of Mato Grosso do Sul. When the assault took place, three months into his prison term at the end of July, he was as yet unaware of the break. He was mixing with the other prisoners and was just coming to the end of his outdoor time when he was surrounded by around twenty members of the PCC. Taken by surprise, he didn't have the time or the instinct to react. He was kicked and beaten, but prison officers stepped in and managed to save from him being lynched.

'It took a while for it to sink in,' he says, his eyes still gleaming with hatred. 'I knew I hadn't screwed up. I hadn't broken any rules. I was jumped because of an acronym.' After the outbreak of conflict between the two groups he felt threatened and betrayed, hearing shouts every day from the other cells and prison wings. He was *encurralado* (cornered or trapped), a term used to refer to gang members in prisons dominated by a rival group.

On the day of the interview Carlos was sharing a cell with a number of other *encurralados*. There were nine of them in all, confined to two minuscule single cells in a separate high-security section – in other words, isolated from the other prisoners – within a prison unit that was also high security, reserved for rapists, paedophiles and those condemned to death under the criminal code. This meant he was effectively under double high security, a condition regarded as humiliating

for a prisoner with his career path and criminal status.

To prevent them from being killed, he and the other prisoners in this group were being kept in a space separated by an iron wall, which had only a small opening to let the air in so they could breathe. Rumours were circulating that there was a bounty on his head, and up to R$50,000 (around $15,000 in 2016) was being offered for his execution. With no outdoor time, restrictions on washing and receiving visitors and absolutely nothing to do, Carlos had reached the end of his tether. His fury intensified when he thought about his wife, who had been attacked in front of the prison while holding their baby of less than a year old. Subject to surveillance in the weeks following the attack, Carlos was unaware that wire taps had discovered his plans for revenge. 'I'm going to make them pay for breaking my teeth,' he said in one recorded conversation.

This conflict was not your average prison brawl but rather marked a major rift in a network that had been developing since the early 1980s, the business of which was the distribution of drugs on the Brazilian market as well as abroad. Over a period of thirty years this network had split into two large groups: the wholesalers (*atacadistas*), who manned the borders to bring drugs in from Paraguay, Bolivia, Peru and Colombia and distribute them within Brazil or transfer them out of the country, and the street dealers (*varejistas*), who sold drugs in their states of origin.

To be a wholesaler demands a cool head and the ability to think on your feet

Above: Children portion out hashish for a group affiliated to the PCC.

to deal with obstacles that appear on the road from the moment the drugs leave the confines of a ranch in Paraguay (for marijuana), or the Andes (for cocaine). Wholesalers need to have access to capital to invest in the merchandise, political savvy to bribe the authorities patrolling the routes, pilot contacts and contingency plans in place to avoid any damages – a set of attributes that makes them the wealthiest and best-prepared class in the drug trade.

Street dealers, on the other hand, are easy targets, disposable, forced to fight over sales in the streets and trade bullets in skirmishes with rivals and the police. In the early decades of drug trafficking two business models determined the trajectory of the street-dealer trade in Brazilian crack houses. One of these appeared in Rio de Janeiro with the emergence of the Comando Vermelho at the end of the 1970s. The CV was the first organised-crime group in urban Brazil, and they began selling drugs through a vertical and hierarchical structure. Spectacular turf wars ensued, complete with heavy weaponry, *favela* invasions, stray bullets and many deaths.

In the rest of Brazil, including São Paulo, the business model was different but no less violent. Small and micro-traffickers were relatively free to use wholesaler sources to open up trading points in their territories. This led to the creation of a street-dealer distribution network in which small groups or individuals would compete in a bloody battle for power and markets, and many of them were killed, often over trivial matters, at the hands of rivals, the police or death squads.

The changes to the network configuration began to intensify in the late 1990s, when the street dealers gained enough experience to advance within the *traficos'* social hierarchy. The first drug-trade impresario who managed to harness the potential of this network was Fernandinho Beira-Mar, affiliated with the CV. He understood the strategic significance of the borders and partnerships with large producers, eliminating the need for intermediaries. In the late 1990s Beira-Mar left Duque de Caxias in Rio's Baixada Fluminense and went to Paraguay and Colombia to set himself up as a wholesaler. His wide network of contacts in the communities in Rio and his good relationships with criminals from São Paulo opened doors for him.

The network took on a new dimension in the 2000s after Beira-Mar was imprisoned. Taking advantage of the CV leader's experience and contacts, the PCC took coordinated action from the jails in São Paulo to approach drug suppliers directly. A new form of technology facilitated this task, which would have been impossible only a few years earlier: the mobile phone. Now inmates could communicate with detainees in other jails and with their allies outside the prison walls. As a result of this shift, prisons became spaces where professional traffickers could coordinate, tapping into a network that had never been so interconnected. The PCC's induction into wholesale dealing and its new forms of criminal organisation sparked a minor revolution in the way drugs were distributed in Brazil.

The PCC also introduced an innovative new discourse. The Paulista group claimed they were carrying out crimes in the name of those who were 'oppressed by the system' rather than defending their own interests, thereby differentiating themselves from the individualism of the carioca traffickers. They declared the existence of a world of crime and illegality in prisons and peripheral regions, known as *quebradas*. For the PCC, crime began to organise itself around an ideology: the profits from the organisation would be used to benefit criminals in general. According to this new philosophy, instead of resorting to self-destruction, criminals should find ways of organising themselves to survive within the system and maximise their profits. One of the maxims of the PCC is 'crime strengthens crime'. The enemies were the police and the *bandidos sangue ruim*, those criminals who failed to abide by the rules imposed by the self-proclaimed 'Party of Crime'.

The money made from drug trafficking would bankroll the bureaucratic structure put in place to defend its members' interests. Cutting out the middle men and going straight to the suppliers of marijuana and cocaine paste was a strategic step towards this goal. It was as if those on the lowest rung of the ladder, who killed and died in droves in Brazilian prisons and peripheral regions, realised that, with a little organisation, they could grab the reins. As the PCC put their plan into action, a new business model for the drug trade began to take shape, and Brazil's criminal underworld stepped up a gear.

The prisons also played a strategic role, in that they facilitated connections between criminal networks across different states. The wholesaler PCC began distributing through street dealers in every state in the country, creating an integrated nationwide illegal drug market. It didn't take long for this network to generate new rivalries and conflicts capable of producing a domino effect. Those who were already members of this world lost their status as free agents. Now the path taken by each individual was tied to the gang to which they belonged.

Carlos, for example, started out in crime in Cuiabá, Mato Grosso, in the early

Monday 15 May 2006. Reports of shops, buses and schools being under attack – as well as rumours that criminal gangs have ordered a curfew – spread throughout the day. No one knows if the reports are true, and the city of São Paulo is brought to a standstill by fear. At 6 p.m. the traffic-management company, CET, reports 218 kilometres of traffic jams after the city's transport system is largely suspended following the torching of numerous buses while in service. A few days earlier more than seven hundred prisoners belonging to the crime organisation Primeiro Comando da Capital (PCC) – including its leader, Marcos Willians Herba Camacho, aka Marcola – had been transferred to maximum-security prisons far from the city. Following this, over the course of just a few hours, there are sixty-four attacks on the police, twenty-five officers killed and simultaneous uprisings in twenty-four prisons – and the violence continues to spread. It is the largest attack launched by organised crime ever recorded in Brazil's history. The police crackdown begins on Sunday, and the counter-attack is brutal. Many are killed. Police target those believed to be criminals but later admit that innocent people may have died. According to rumours that circulate in the press, the ceasefire – after around 140 deaths and more than fifty wounded – comes after an 'agreement' between the police, the authorities and the leaders of the factions. No one has ever admitted that any such deal was ever struck.

2000s, a time when a criminal career was limited to working with a few accomplices and contacts. He was charged with armed robbery and earned a degree of respect from robbing banks, a crime that demanded a high level of planning and coordination. In prison he was seen as a fearless and violent inmate, but he acted alone and had few allies. He was part of a network with limited connections. Despite his confrontational disposition, he was vulnerable because he was isolated.

His advancement within the world of crime began after he joined the branch of the Comando Vermelho in Mato Grosso, where he rose to a leadership position. The CV was relatively new to the region; the local CV-MT had been created in 2013 by a former ally of the PCC called Sandro da Silva Rabelo, known as Sandro Louco (Crazy Sandro). Sandro joined the CV after serving time at Mossoró Federal Prison alongside Fernandinho Beira-Mar. The CV offered an advantage over the Paulista group because they guaranteed the Mato Grosso criminals financial and organisational autonomy. The CV started gaining ground in the state, recruiting almost three thousand members to become Mato Grosso's dominant criminal gang. The order to teach Carlos a lesson came from a prison unit in the neighbouring state of Mato Grosso do Sul a month after the PCC sent the message announcing their break with the CV. Attacking rivals in this state was a safe action for the PCC, who had exercised a strong influence over the region since the early 2000s and controlled the local system.

*

An experienced armed robber with more than forty prosecutions to his name in various cities across the state of São Paulo, Moreno had enough of a track record to assume a leadership role. When he was sent to the border regions his mission was to organise the import of drugs through Paraguay and Bolivia for the PCC. He ended up in prison in 2013 and played a key role in running the PCC's operations from inside the jails of Mato Grosso do Sul. Moreno was one of the most active members of the Sintonia dos Estados e Países – one of the highest-ranking operation units in the command structure developed over the years by the PCC, the role of which was to coordinate the running of the network outside São Paulo – and he was therefore one of the key figures responsible for the conflicts that followed.

The Paulista bosses were well aware of the damage a conflict with the CV could cause. In June 2016 Moreno tried to explain that there had been no declaration of war from the PCC. Breaking the pact was more a show of force from the Paulista group, necessary to let their rivals know who really set the rules of crime in Brazil. 'The CV is not our enemy, we are just no longer allies,' he reflected. Although he confirmed the PCC's desire to extend their reach throughout the country, he denied this could trigger a war: 'Not a war, but there could be a clash of ideas.' Moreno and the PCC underestimated their rivals' capacity to mobilise; the CV accepted the challenge and prepared for a fight. The equilibrium of this new network, interconnected at a national level, would be put to the test in determining how the rivals would defend themselves against the power of the PCC.

Confined to the same cell as Carlos and the other prisoners in the high-security unit, Paulo arrived at his interview looking calmer than Carlos, with the serenity of someone who was not yet a target but was aware of the risk he was running. He was also prepared to talk about what went on behind the scenes of the conflict as he

Above: A police officer injured during a demonstration against the fare increases on public transport in São Paulo, 2013.
Below: A protester confronts the police in São Paolo.

Above: A young man suspected of house-breaking is arrested by São Paulo police.
Below: A crack user during a police operation to clamp down on dealers in São Paolo.

Above: A young man is arrested on suspicion of stealing a car, while his mother cries as the police take him away **(below)**.

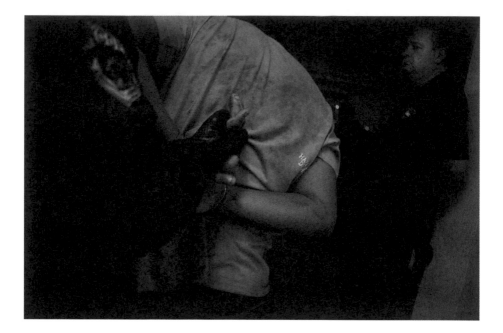

This page: Suspects arrested after an attempted bank robbery in São Paulo.

tried to explain how neither he nor his allies were responsible for the war that was about to break out. Paulo was not just any prisoner; he was one of the leaders of the Primeiro Grupo Catarinense (PGC), a rival of the PCC in Santa Catarina. Like the majority of prisoners who belong to gangs, especially those who held prominent positions in the hierarchy, he displayed certain attributes that set him apart from the incarcerated masses: intelligence and the ability to articulate his reasoning; knowledge of his basic rights; a general understanding of the situation; and the capacity to analyse the imminent tragedy.

Conflicts between the PCC and the PGC were nothing new. Since as early as 2009 the Paulistas had been trying to convince the Catarinense group of the importance of mutual solidarity and collaboration. This, however, was seen by the Catarinense criminals as an arrogant attempt at domination, the strong imposing on the weak. In practice, joining up with the PCC meant adopting its rules and integrating local criminals into the crime network controlled from the prisons in São Paulo. As the PGC resisted the Paulistas' voracious appetite for expansion, the relationship defined by the PCC as one of respect and coexistence gradually deteriorated. It is not known when exactly the PCC formulated a plan to take over Santa Catarina, since the flow of drugs to the foreign markets via the port of Itajaí was always a trigger for conflict. The struggle for trade and power, however, didn't threaten the coexistence of the members of these two groups. Peace reigned in the jails, despite mounting regional rivalries.

Back in the prison in Mato Grosso do Sul, Paulo was complaining about the retaliations he'd been subjected to. He thought he had shown respect after five years in another prison living alongside prisoners from the PCC. He was surprised by the outbreak of violence, but he had been segregated in time and had managed to escape unscathed. He felt disrespected, as a criminal who had always abided by the rules of crime. Serving the rest of his sentence under high security was humiliating. The new circumstances created dangerous spaces, with ambushes on all sides. In Mato Grosso do Sul the group of nine prisoners in the high-security wing had enemies who had been expelled from the PCC. Paulo believed these ex-PCCs would accept the mission to kill them in an attempt to be pardoned and readmitted to the ranks. 'I want to go to another state, like Mato Grosso or Santa Catarina. There, it's the PCC who are in the minority,' he said.

At just over forty years of age, Paulo had, over two decades, accumulated a wealth of criminal experience, serving jail sentences in Santa Catarina – his home state – Rio Grande do Sul, São Paulo, Paraná and Mato Grosso do Sul. A month before the riots he listed the armed alliances facing off against the PCC. As well as the PGC and the CV, he cited the Família do Norte (FDN) from Amazonas and the Sindicato do Crime from Rio Grande do Norte. 'States in the Northeast and Central-West are arming themselves to combat the PCC with help from groups from neighbouring countries. The PCC had been infiltrating several states and wanted to stamp out the other Brazilian groups, so the CV started playing a game of chess, allying itself with the smaller groups,' he explains.

In 2014 the pieces on this chessboard started to shift inside the prisons. The PCC made the first move, realising that control of the drug market was linked to consolidating its power within the penal system. With the gang leaders behind bars, guaranteeing their integrity was an urgent and strategic objective. This instigated a kind of cold war, with the Paulistas boosting their numbers in various prison units across Brazil by 'baptising' new members. The term baptism gives a sense of what this affiliation means: new members must 'convert' to the rules laid down by the gang. Members would lose their autonomy and be subject to moral and financial commitments, but they gained protection and privileges through belonging to the group – lawyers who could speed up the progress of a sentence, loans of weaponry and capital for new crimes, a broad network of drug-supplier contacts and defence against rivals. Seeking to increase the size of the membership and recruit troops for the impending war, rules for new PCC members were relaxed. Instead of requiring three *padrinhos* – guarantors who would take responsibility for any potential slip-ups on the part of the individual – as is the case in São Paulo, one would now be enough. The *cebola* (onion) – the term for the monthly fee the PCC demands from its members outside the prisons – was also reduced. This sum, which in São Paulo ranges between R$700 and R$1,000 (c. $315–450 in 2014), was lowered to R$400 (c. $180) to be more in keeping with the economic realities for criminals in other states. At the height of the war, in order to control states where the conflict was raging – Ceará, for instance – the *cebola* payments were temporarily suspended. Targets were also set for certain states, instructing them to recruit hundreds of new members.

The strategy was a success. New members were recorded by state intelligence in the prisons and by groups combating organised crime from the public prosecution service. According to their calculations, at the end of 2012 the PCC had around 2,400 prisoners spread across twenty-four states – the exceptions were

Roraima, Rondônia and Amapá. In the state of São Paulo there were around eight thousand members – 80 per cent of them in prison. Over the next two years membership across the country climbed slowly, and the PCC gained 3,200 members in 2013 and 2014, the year the strategy of mass occupation started to be implemented.

In the four years leading up to 2018 the PCC recruited eighteen thousand members (three thousand in São Paulo state and fifteen thousand elsewhere) bringing the total to more than twenty-nine thousand across Brazil, with representatives in every state. In Ceará, for example, membership jumped from seventy-seven in 2012 to 2,500, making it the state with the third-highest number of PCC members in the country, behind São Paulo which had close to eleven thousand and a little below Paraná. Roraima, which in 2012 had no PCC presence at all, passed a thousand members, and Rondônia hit nearly eight hundred. Along with the new members, rules arrived in the jails that had been forged years previously in the criminal context of São Paulo.

In certain regions, the Paulistas acquired a reputation for being overbearing, arrogant and oppressive, outsiders who didn't respect local customs. This was the case in Rio Grande do Norte, where the Sindicato do Crime capitalised on the discontent provoked by the rules and general attitude of the PCC. Part of their offensive inside the prisons called for a ban on the use of crack and cocaine paste in the jails, in a repeat of the rule that had successfully contributed towards reducing conflict in the prisons of São Paulo. In the state of Roraima the ban was announced in a November 2013 message to the Penitenciária Agrícola de Monte Cristo, at a time when the faction was starting to be more active in the local penal system.

Salve to all / Prison unit

PA

We, the Sintônia Geral of the state of RR send our greetings to you all, brothers and comrades, and embrace you firmly, loyally and sincerely. We congratulate all our brothers and comrades for the proud alliance that is developing in this unit, in this region and in this system today, which is the PA prison unit.

We are announcing the ban of the use of crack and cocaine paste, which enslaves the human being and the world of crime through its negative effects on the personality and character, as the sintônia of the state of RR.

Taking all of you into consideration, brothers and comrades, we declare via this message that from 10/11/2013 the sale and use of crack and cocaine paste will be banned in all prison systems in the region and in the PA unit. We know the struggle will be great, but together we shall succeed.

The *milícias* are now the main criminal presence in Rio de Janeiro, if not in numbers then certainly by their ability to organise. They have spread into numerous *favelas*, where they have replaced the long-standing clans such as the Comando Vermelho and the Terceiro Comando. And yet the *milícias* are a recent phenomenon. In the early 2000s they were known as community self-defence groups and were composed, as they still are today, of policemen, firemen, vigilantes and members of the army. They told people they were there to tackle the drug traffickers. In the echoing void left by the state, however, they very quickly became the oppressors, using extortion and intimidation and demanding 'taxes' on transport, (pirate) cable TV, gas supplies and business. And later they, too, turned to trafficking weapons and drugs. They have spread like a virus. According to figures published by the webzine *The Intercept Brasil*, they are now present in at least thirty-seven districts and 167 *favelas*. Around two million people in Rio live under their control. In the most run-down areas of the city they control their territory with an iron fist, and this soon attracted interest from politicians, so these districts became valuable reservoirs of votes exposed to corruption. As a result, the *milícias* have radically altered the political face of the city, penetrating right into the heart of the legislative assembly that governs Rio. According to investigators, the murder of Marielle Franco in March 2018 was planned by those involved with the *milícias* because they saw her exposure of wrongdoing as a threat to their business interests.

Banning the sale of crack and cocaine paste within the system blocked a major source of revenue for traffickers in these states. For this and a number of other reasons the discontent began to spread. Paulo described how at this point the 'CV joins forces with the local traffickers, who don't want a dictator. The PCC wants to rule alone. As well as giving orders, they impose "real estate" partnerships where members have to pay R$700 (*c.* $315) a month. The PGV and the CV don't make them pay anything. So this consolidates relations with the local population.' (This refers to the way the different factions interact with the 'locals', whether at the borders or inside prison units in other states.)

Paulo explained how the PCC's rivals were receiving assistance from other South American groups who were uncomfortable with the Paulistas' expansion and capacity for organisation. 'Brazil has a cartel, but each state also has its own. When they need reinforcements, the CV sends them,' he explains. Recently the CV had seen an increase in requests for support. According to leaders of the PGC, the Paulistas had already blocked the activities of other Brazilian gangs in Paraná, one of the most important states for the import of drugs into the country, where the PCC dominated the prisons and the drug market. The next step would be to block Mato Grosso do Sul, the continent's main drug corridor.

The leaders of the PGC were able to evaluate how different penal policies applied across the states could give rise to unequal criminal opportunities. Paulo knew that the leaders of other factions were at a disadvantage compared with the Paulistas because of the long periods they spent in the Federal Penitentiary System (SPF) where communications were difficult, especially with the outside world, which compromised the criminal activities of gangs like the CV and the PGC. 'Why is Marcola [the leader of the PCC] the only one not in a federal prison?' he repeated several times. 'Tell me, why do all the gangs have leaders in federal prisons except the PCC?' He remained unconvinced by the fact that in December 2016 the PCC bosses were moved to the Regime Disciplinar Diferenciado (Special Disciplinar Programme) in the Centro de Readaptação Penitenciária (Penitentiary Readaptation Centre) in Presidente Bernardes, a Paulista maximum-security unit. 'I'll only believe it when Marcola goes to federal prison. As long as he stays in São Paulo, I'm not buying it.'

On the other hand, the PCC's absence in the federal prisons facilitated collusions between regional gangs and the CV, who became the immediate point of reference for requests for aid in resisting the expansion of the PCC. The recruitment drive inside the prisons placed an unbearable strain on the system between 2014 and 2017. Meanwhile, the state governors and authorities failed to act, and the information was kept well away from the media spotlight and entirely absent from public debate.

In the shadows, far from the newspaper headlines, isolated incidents of violence and death began to take place across Brazil. In the rush to arms, the rivals, as expected, also began to organise themselves and form alliances. Once the break between the factions was declared, the groups formed a cartel. 'The CV, the FDN and the PGC are now all one family,' says Paulo. Each group is autonomous, but they share part of the national prison system and the drug market in opposition to the PCC. The three gangs formed alliances with small local groups, who also opposed the hegemonic project of the Paulistas.

They were joined by the Sindicato do Crime from Rio Grande do Norte, Bonde dos 40 from Maranhão and Okaida from Paraíba. In this game of chess the PCC also realised the importance of forming alliances and established partnerships with the Guardiões do Estado from Ceará, Bonde dos 13 from Acre, Bonde dos 30 from Pará and the Estados Unidos from Paraíba. War was declared, and the rival factions took their positions.

Coordinated alliances in crime had been shaping the new criminal landscape in Brazil, which rapidly divided around these two large groups. When the CV was founded in the late 1970s its motto 'Peace, Justice and Liberty' opposed prison oppression and social injustice. In time this would serve as a reference point for the foundation of the Paulista group, and the PCC, when it emerged from the prisons in São Paulo over a decade later, used the same motto, and its first charter even declared in writing its 'coalition' with the carioca group. The alliance was never formalised in terms of a shared programme, but it functioned for two decades through the commercial cooperation and protection and peaceful coexistence of the membership of both organisations.

Before definitively breaking with the CV, the PCC tried playing a final card with its historic allies, sending a message to the leader of the CV in Rio de Janeiro, Marcinho VP, who was detained in the federal prison of Catanduvas in Paraná. The faction maintained its diplomatic approach, faithful to the philosophy of avoiding conflict and seeking to bring about criminal unity. The message was sent from Presidente Venceslau, where the PCC bosses were based.

The PCC members' request for clarification was met with indifference. As Marcinho VP himself would say, by way of

Salve – this message is for Marcinho VP of the CV, who is now in federal prison at Catanduvas. We send our regards.

We are writing to ask for clarification on your part, because you told us to be aware of the false prophets followed by our brothers in federal prisons, and you also said you would not be baptising anyone in federal prison to avoid these kinds of problems.

But we have also learned that you are baptising in the federal prisons and that those people you are baptising are going back to their states of origin, and when they get there they are baptising others, even our enemies, and they're also protecting people we have condemned to death, situations like this, and these people you have baptised want to prevent us from baptising in these states and we will never allow this.

There are some factions in these states who want to fight us, they say they have made alliances with you and that their enemy is your enemy. We don't know what this means, which is why we want clarification from you, because up to now you have been our friends and we have great respect for you, and you know our objective is to unite criminals all over the country, where crime strengthens crime in peace, justice, liberty and unity.

This is your last chance, we want you to take a position, we want clarification from your side, we want to be clear that we respect your choice, but we are not going to tolerate what has been going on. We are doing our part in contacting you first, now it is your turn.

Sending you our regards,

SIGNED: Sintonia final dos estados

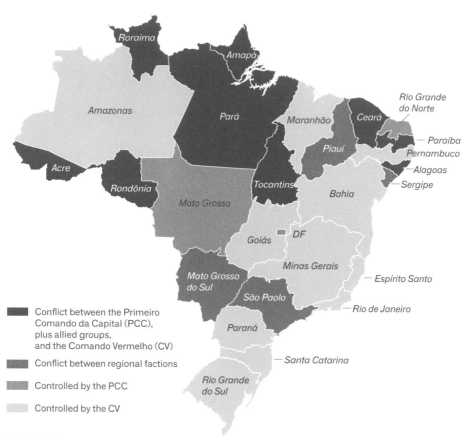

Conflict between the Primeiro
Comando da Capital (PCC),
plus allied groups,
and the Comando Vermelho (CV)

Conflict between regional factions

Controlled by the PCC

Controlled by the CV

SOURCE: UOL

ETHNICITY AND AGE GROUPS OF DRUG DEALERS IN RIO'S FAVELAS

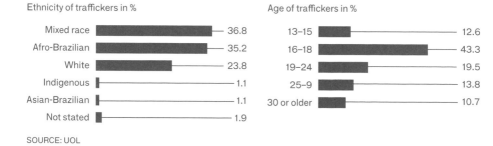

Ethnicity of traffickers in %

Mixed race	36.8
Afro-Brazilian	35.2
White	23.8
Indigenous	1.1
Asian-Brazilian	1.1
Not stated	1.9

Age of traffickers in %

13–15	12.6
16–18	43.3
19–24	19.5
25–9	13.8
30 or older	10.7

SOURCE: UOL

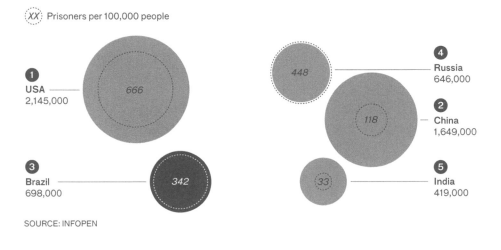

XX Prisoners per 100,000 people

1 USA 2,145,000 — 666

3 Brazil 698,000 — 342

448

118

33

4 Russia 646,000

2 China 1,649,000

5 India 419,000

SOURCE: INFOPEN

justification, they had no control over the regional leaders, who acted autonomously without seeking authorisation from any central command. That was when the PCC decided to go on the offensive, declaring their break with the CV in their message of June 2016.

In August 2016, one month after Carlos was assaulted, the PCC led an uprising at the maximum-security prison in Naviraí, Mato Grosso do Sul, about four hundred kilometres from Campo Grande. Three prisoners who were supposedly linked to the CV were killed, one of them decapitated. Buses were set on fire. At the end of the riots a video was recorded by a prisoner saying, 'everyone will die' and 'all the regions will be destroyed'. The footage was shared by other prisoners and outside the prisons via WhatsApp, which would become the main platform for broadcasting the barbarism to come.

The new prison structure began to be revealed with all its colours and flags. Brazilian intelligence services identified eighty gangs acting out of the prisons, while the authorities failed to debate the issue, unaware of the relevance of these groups. When the conflict broke out they were totally unprepared to deal with the situation. It's difficult to say whether the war was planned by the PCC or whether they were taking diplomatic steps to avoid it, but over the months that followed it became clear that the situation was running out of control. ✒

View of the Rocinha *favela*,
Rio de Janeiro.

You've Got Mail!

FABIAN FEDERL
Translated by Stephen Smithson

There was a time when the streets of Rocinha had no addresses, but then Eliane Ramos drew the first map of the area, which she used for her postal start-up. A success story from the *favela*.

177

Despite the midday summer sun, the alleyways of Rocinha are pitch dark. A thin ray of sunshine will occasionally enter this Rio de Janeiro *favela* through a vacant lot, penetrating its labyrinth of nooks, alleys, corners and tunnels. Or one of the *becos* (as the narrowest alleys – narrower than an individual arm span – are called in Portuguese) will receive artificial light from the window display of a bakery. The air is stagnant; the stench of the open sewers – which transport the effluent of hundreds of thousands of residents down the hill – wafts through the streets.

Eliane Ramos Vieira da Silva, a woman in her late forties with straight, dark hair and a sprinkling of freckles, was born here and grew up in these *becos*. With her elegant clothes – blouse and tapered trousers, not the kind of outfit normally worn in these parts – she stands out. With hasty steps Eliane takes us through the neighbourhood. Reaching the end of a tunnel of houses we emerge abruptly from the *beco* to find ourselves standing, blinded by the sudden brightness, before a football pitch surrounded by concrete walls. Nelson José da Silva, who accompanies Eliane, signals to us to wait and runs on ahead.

At the entrance to one of the *becos*, a dozen or so youths of around fifteen or sixteen years of age sit on two sofas. Each wears headphones, and each is bare chested with a walkie-talkie in the waistband of his swimming trunks. These young men control the area on behalf of one of the drug lords. Nelson goes up to them, makes a gesture of reassurance, turns around and gives a thumbs-up. The young men are acting tough because of us – we are strangers – but the presence of Nelson and Eliane does not worry them; quite the opposite, in fact, for these lads rely upon them, as do a large number of Rocinha residents.

Nelson is a courier for a private postal service serving Rocinha, and Eliane is its boss. And just as it's normal for the post to be delivered in Zurich, Berlin or Paris, it's normal for it not to arrive in Rocinha. Residents have no addresses; the *becos* have no names – or, worse still, several different names. House numbers are assigned geographically in one place, chronologically in another and completely arbitrarily everywhere. The little alleyways develop organically: one person builds a wall and another builds a tunnel or some steps, and the street system is altered completely. Brazil's state postal system made no attempt at first to find a solution; Rocinha's inhabitants simply did not receive any post. This meant no credit cards, no pension notifications and no legal way of obtaining an electricity supply.

Eliane Ramos Vieira da Silva had lived her entire life without receiving a single letter until one day she decided that this wasn't the way things had to be. Together with her husband and cousin she set up a firm, Carteiro Amigo – the Friendly Postman – and changed the lives of tens of thousands of *favela* dwellers at a stroke. For a small fee subscribers can be just as confident that their letters and parcels will reach them as are residents in one of Rio's more conventional areas. Within just a few years Carteiro Amigo expanded into other areas similar to

FABIAN FEDERL is a freelance journalist originally from France who lives and works between Berlin, Lisbon and Rio de Janeiro. He writes for the newspapers *Süddeutsche Zeitung* and *Der Tagesspiegel* as well as the weekly magazine *Die Zeit*. His investigations have been published by titles such as *Elle*, *Brand Eins*, *Reportagen*, *Internazionale* and *Libération*.

Above: Entering Rocinha.

Rocinha, and it's now probably the most successful business ever to have been set up in a *favela*. 'Having an address makes *favela* dwellers into citizens,' says Eliane. 'Being able to receive your post is a basic right,' she insists.

Rocinha, Portuguese for little farmstead, covers a hillside in the south of Rio. With around 250,000 inhabitants, it's a major part of the city. The view across the beach of São Conrado – granite rocks rising up abruptly out of the rainforest, the statue of Christ the Redeemer to the rear – is one of the city's, if not the world's, most beautiful. A single thoroughfare that can properly be called a road, the Estrada da Gávea, runs through the *favela* in serpentine lines from the metro station near the beach to high up in the Atlantic Forest, over the hill and into the affluent parts of Rio's South Zone.

Rocinha is divided up into several neighbourhoods named after streets that lead off from Estrada da Gávea to form a herringbone pattern. Rocinha is essentially uncharted terrain – Google Maps lists only a handful of streets. The navigation systems used by taxi and Uber drivers can find their way only to the foot of the hill or to addresses along the Estrada – which, for this reason, is where Rocinha's public life is lived: bars and restaurants, shops selling car parts, iron goods, building materials next to fashion stores, drug stores, pharmacies. Everywhere people are chatting, smoking; men in overalls lean against the walls of houses, and, when the sun is shining, everyone who can stands in the shade beside the dense housing. Thousands of *mototaxis* race honking across the Estrada; buses carrying out impossible manoeuvres become wedged in

FAVELAS

On the subject of the *favelas*, myth and reality merge – starting with the term itself, which may have been derived from a rash-causing plant growing on the hills of Rio that lent its name to Favela, the original *comunidade*. But the first to really develop was perhaps the Morro da Providência, which still exists in the port area of Rio. In the late 19th century veterans of the civil conflict known as the War of Canudos arrived there, almost all of them black former slaves. The urban reform brought in by the mayor, Pereira Passos, in the early 20th century did the rest, transferring the poor occupants of the city centre's crumbling housing blocks to the higher ground. To this day, myth and reality shape the life of the *comunidades*, or *morros*, or *favelas*. How many people live there? Are they really so dangerous? What is their economy like? In Brazil, nowhere suffers from more misunderstanding, lack of knowledge and prejudice than the *favelas*. According to

the 2010 census run by the Brazilian Institute of Geography and Statistics (IBGE), there are around a thousand in Rio, home to 22 per cent of the city's population. But in reality it is impossible to produce a true statistical picture. If it weren't for an informal census carried out by a few NGOs in the Complexo da Maré, as reported in *The Economist* in 2019, we would know almost nothing about that *favela*. The lack of information affects all the *comunidades*, beginning with Rocinha, even though it is the one that has attracted the most attention and is one of the largest in South America, a genuine city in its own right with its own cultural life, artists, businesses, restaurants and schools. And the same goes for the others: Vidigal, Prazeres, São Carlos, Corõa, Juramento, Cabrito, Mangueira, Jacarezinho, Cidade de Deus and the agglomerations like Maré and Alemão. Each of them is at the same time urban centre and suburb, and they are certainly the places where the fastest and most significant social changes are taking place in the country.

the bends. Hardly anybody turns into the side-streets – too narrow, too meandering, too confusing; even experienced drivers get lost in them. Only the locals know their way around, and even they know no more than they need to.

Its singular geography and culture have made Rocinha impenetrable for most outsiders. Service providers – post, waste disposal, internet – have never managed to establish themselves, nor have electricity or water utilities. Two-thirds of residents obtain electricity, internet and water by illegal means. Waste is flushed down from the top of the hill into the sea. Rocinha is nevertheless a functioning micro-economy. You can get anything here, albeit by alternative means. Like the other people who live in the *favela*, Eliane knows the rules. She identified a need and made it her business – and her life's work – to meet it.

'These stairs here were built by my father,' says Eliane, and she waves us over to concrete steps into a *beco* in the middle of Rocinha. Eliane speaks loud and fast, her voice picking up speed when something is important, as though there is not enough time for so many words.

Eliane knocks against the concrete wall of a little house painted in many colours. Washing hangs on rails on the veranda; the scent of detergent mixes with the musty air of the narrow streets. She was born in this house in 1972 and spent her childhood and youth there. Eliane's father did not build only stairs but also the house and the *becos*. The *beco* outside his front door he called Travessa Vieira after the family name; he gave each of the other *becos* names of places in the Bible:

Travessa Samaritana, Travessa Jordão, Travessa Galileia.

Eliane's family is, like most families in Rocinha, evangelical; they are devout believers. Eliane is one of nine sisters. Her parents arrived in Rio as migrant workers from Brazil's poor Northeast. Her mother found a job in a kindergarten at the foot of the hill; her father worked wherever work could be found – as a bus driver, market trader, building labourer. At eighteen Eliane left school and started a degree course. From seven in the morning until late in the afternoon she would help out in the kindergarten, and then she would travel into town where she would attend a teacher-training course until ten at night. But Eliane did not want to become a teacher. She was interested in business studies, in planning and organisation – and yes, in money. She taught herself the basics of business studies, increasingly neglecting her teaching course until, despite strong protest from her mother, she dropped out in the sixth semester.

Eliane leads us past more concrete walls and railings, through labyrinths of *becos*, some of them almost completely dark, closed off from above. These follow the typical construction pattern of the *favelas*. The first generation builds on the ground floor; the next adds a first floor, extending the boundaries a little to add a few square metres. The same happens in the house opposite, so that by the third generation the house walls meet in the middle, making the *beco* into a tunnel. Eliane appears captivated, pauses again and looks at the passages in front of her. She then turns to us and says, 'All of this here was rainforest back then.'

Although born here, Eliane seems not to belong; she's like an outsider. She wears jewellery she has designed herself and brand-name shoes – not ostentatious but

THE PASSENGER   Fabian Federl

tasteful. Her demeanour – the controlled manner in which she speaks, her sophisticated vocabulary, her good manners and politeness – is that of somebody who has made her way out of the *favela*. A few years ago she moved out of Rocinha into the middle-class Jacarepagua neighbourhood, and bit by bit she moved her whole family with her. But Eliane has never forgotten that she comes from Rocinha – and she is proud of her roots.

At the busiest corner at the foot of Rocinha lies the Carteiro Amigo office. The furnishing is sparse – a desk with a telephone and a computer, a dividing wall behind which the parcels and letters are stored. An agent of the Brazilian postal service enters the office; Eliane greets him, a phone pressed between her shoulder and her ear. The courier lays a deep pile of letters on the desk. Nelson takes it and begins to sort them, working out the best delivery route. Nelson reckons that he knows 90 per cent of subscribers' addresses by heart. Only rarely does he look something up on the system. This system, Eliane's computerised record of the addresses, is the reason for the company's success. More than simply bringing order to the address system, Carteiro Amigo created that system and the addresses themselves. And it drew a map from this information.

The history of this map begins in the summer of 2000, when Eliane had just had her first son, Pedro Junior. The Brazilian state was preparing to carry out a census, which was going to include the *favelas* of Rio de Janeiro. Thousands of helpers were needed, so Eliane and her husband Pedro applied. Her cousin Sila joined them.

With their clipboards and questionnaires they ran through the *becos* of the Vila Cruzeiro, affectionately known as Vila Miséria, far up in the Rochinha. After they had visited just the first few houses it became clear to the three of them that the questionnaires could not be made to work there. The address section alone was impossible to complete. The residents of one *beco*, for example, said that the registered official street name was Rua 5, while the electricity suppliers called it Rua 10; the residents themselves, however, referred to it as Beco dos Espancados. Three different names for the same place.

Instead of house numbers the residents used descriptions, such as 'three houses from the *boteco*', 'the house with the black door and the Jesus plaque' or 'the door next to the mango tree'. For Eliane, Pedro and Sila, who had grown up in Rocinha, there was nothing unusual in this way of doing things. The office of statistics, however, found it impossible to manage. The three therefore began to draw up a map on which they marked the houses they had visited with the survey forms. In this way they produced a complete map of the Vila Cruzeiro over the following days. They retained the street names used by the inhabitants; house numbers they allocated themselves, starting from the main street and moving away from it in ascending order.

While going around the Vila Cruzeiro, Eliane would frequently see small wooden crates filled with letters simply left by the roadside. She hardly noticed them; this was how the Brazilian postal service normally delivered letters here. So many times in her life Eliane had seen letters soaked through, boxes chucked about, envelopes torn open.

Pages 182–3: A view across Rio de Janeiro from Rocinha.
Right: A resident of the *favela* receives a letter at his home.

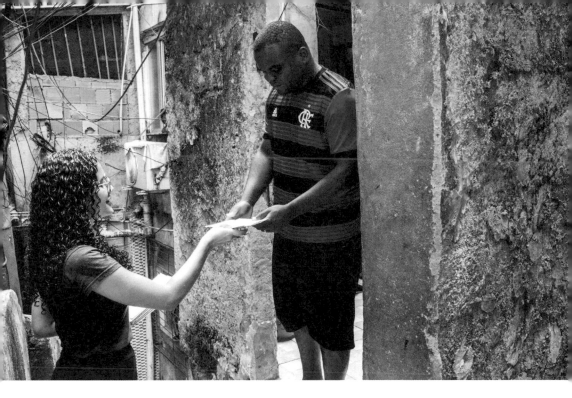

Eliane can no longer remember which of them first came up with the idea, but it was while undertaking the census that the three of them started to carry around small flyers that they had printed themselves – flyers advertising a reliable delivery service for letters and parcels. A few months later this would develop into Carteiro Amigo.

Eliane used the time she was spending at home with her newborn child to get the business up and running. She rented a tiny business premises on the Estrada da Gávea, just two by three metres but easy for the postal service to reach. Carteiro Amigo subscribers could then give this new office as their address and be confident that this would suffice for their letters to reach them. Eliane digitalised the hand-drawn map and developed a formal classification system. In the beginning Pedro and Sila, both of whom at the time worked for a cleaning company, delivered the letters

themselves after work. After nine months both men decided that this side project should become their sole occupation. They left their jobs and took on two delivery agents, one of whom was Nelson, and they hoped for the best. It would have to work out. Eliane says today that, although she believed in the idea, she still had to pray regularly for success. There were, after all, good reasons why scarcely a single business had been able to establish itself in the *favela*.

Eliane stands before the office and calls a *mototaxi* for herself and then two more – one for each of us. We race up the Rocinha hill, over knee-deep potholes and along the narrowest of winding roads, overtaking school buses and several times narrowly avoiding colliding with other *mototaxis*. On a bend halfway up the hill Eliane stops; she wants to show us something. 'There, just ahead,' she says and points across the street – not with her finger but with

a nod of her head – 'is Rua 2.' The current centre of drug trafficking. Dozens of police officers stand in front of the entrance to the *beco*, all of whom stay where they are and make no move against the *bandidos*. 'Each one remains in position,' says Eliane. *Bandidos* and police do not cross one another's path – and residents avoid both. That neither side presents problems for Carteiro Amigo borders on the miraculous.

Paying for protection is an everyday occurrence, and local barons or corrupt police officers in some *favelas* have attempted to extort money from Carteiro Amigo. It has made a brave stand, and of its eleven offices in *favelas* outside Rocinha five have had to close.

'We never had problems of this kind in Rocinha, thank God,' says Eliane. Her company's problem there was of a quite different nature. 'The Brazilian postal service saw us not as an ally,' she says, 'but as a

rival,' as somebody trying to show them up on their own turf, making fools of them.

At the time Carteiro Amigo was set up the postal service's practice for Rocinha was to store letters at the foot of the hill or sometimes to take them further up and then leave them in those wooden crates from which anyone could help themselves. Parcels for Rocinha, meanwhile, were left in post offices in the Leblon or Jardim Botânico districts, both of which were a half-hour away. This meant an expensive trip for any Rocinha resident wanting to collect a package.

While Carteiro Amigo was soon able to get letter deliveries running smoothly and without hassle, parcels continued to present problems. For the first few months the company collected parcels by motorbike courier. Then the manager of the post office branch in Leblon decided to ban this practice on security grounds. This led Eliane, Pedro and Sila to start hiring small vans. As Carteiro Amigo grew, so did the numbers of parcels addressed to the Carteiro Amigo office. The Leblon branch manager started to outsource parcel storage to Ipanema, a further twenty minutes away. Another would allow collection in person only, accepting no proxies. 'Pure obstruction,' says Eliane.

By now local media were starting to take notice of Carteiro Amigo. This, too, was not to the liking of one of the postal service's branch managers. A few days after Pedro had appeared in a big report broadcast by Globo TV, Carteiro Amigo received a telephone call. If any of them should give one more television interview, Pedro was told, the branch manager would personally see to it that parcels would from now on end up in Copacabana, another thirty minutes further away from Rocinha.

Eliane and her co-founders ultimately prevailed against the state-run company. They did this by playing along all the way until they had become so famous that even the most vengeful branch manager would have made a fool of himself if he had kept up the fight. Now Carteiro Amigo has been awarded prizes by the City of Rio de Janeiro, the Brazilian Ministry of Labour and the Social Enterprise World Forum. In 2012, when Carteiro Amigo expanded into another of Rio's slum areas, the financial magazine *Exame* described it as the 'first franchise business to come out of a *favela*'.

As public interest grew, Eliane retreated further into the background and Pedro became the public face of Carteiro Amigo.

He led journalists through Rocinha, gave interviews, posed for photographs; he gave lectures at universities, museums and charitable foundations; he became a public figure within Rocinha, and in 2018 even ran for parliament. Meanwhile, Eliane sat in the office and continued to work on company development. She started to provide business advice for the *favela*. Whenever an investor or promoter was planning anything in Rocinha, advice would be sought from Eliane on key issues: where are the problem areas; how do you deal with the *bandidos* and the police?

Carteiro Amigo started to offer courier services and deliver promotional materials. And it continued to expand. At the end of 2018 the mayor of the rich resort town of Búzios made a telephone call to Pedro. He asked if Carteiro Amigo could advise his local postal service because even he, the mayor, had no reliable way of getting his mail. Pedro once received a query from Google about the possibility of using the Carteiro Amigo map for Google Maps. Pedro's answer? 'Make your own!'

A delivery round lasting roughly two hours, in which he has taken three *moto-taxi* rides and hundreds of steps, ends with Nelson in a particularly stuffy *beco* fanning himself with a letter. He gives a short shake of a rusty iron grill and calls through the opening, '*Ô correio!*' – 'Post!' A woman peeps out of the window on the first floor and calls, 'Coming, coming!' She extends her hand out through the grille; Nelson passes her the letter.

Eliane goes to the door. 'Good day. How are you? I am Eliane, Nelson's boss. Today I'm accompanying him on his rounds to ask if everything is going well and you are satisfied with the service.'

The woman goes up to Eliane, greets her with a kiss on the left and right cheeks, smiles and nods. 'We are like a family.' 🖋

'On the River, I Was King'

The construction of the Belo Monte Dam meant that the men, women and children who were living happily on the banks of the Xingu River had to be relocated to the outskirts of Altamira, one of Brazil's most violent cities. Now they live behind barred windows surrounded by gun violence, forced to buy food with money they never used to have and for which they never before felt the need. Their situation is dire, but the fight back has begun.

ELIANE BRUM
Translated by Diane Grosklaus Whitty

Left: A view of the Pinheiros River, São Paulo.

Antonio das Chagas and Dulcineia Dias had an island, a slice of the Amazon rainforest on the Xingu River. 'I had a better life than anyone in São Paulo,' says Chagas, referring to Brazil's wealthiest city. 'If I wanted to work my land, I did. If I didn't, the land would be there the next day. If I wanted to fish, I did, but if I'd rather pick açaí, I did. I had a river, I had woods, I had tranquillity. On the island, I didn't have any doors. I had a place ... And on the island, we didn't get sick.'

The couple now rent a house with one window. The window has bars because they live on the periphery of Altamira, designated Brazil's second-most violent city. They have discovered hunger, which they cannot find words to describe. When asked to do so, Chagas, a sixty-year-old man who had known nothing of city life before, finds his eyes welling up. Dias, fifty-two, crouches in a corner, her back pressed hard against a cracked cement wall.

Somewhere between their island on the river and their rented house in the city, these people of the forest were converted into urban poor. Typifying the government-led settlement of the Amazon, this process reached its apex under the 1964–85 dictatorship, when mega-projects like the Trans-Amazonian Highway were launched. But the event that obstructed the lives of Chagas, Dias and hundreds of families living on the Xingu took place under democracy.

Built in the Amazon forest, in the state of Pará, the Belo Monte hydroelectric complex is one of the biggest infrastructure projects on the planet. It is also hugely controversial. The Public Prosecutor's Office has filed twenty-four lawsuits against Belo Monte for human rights and environmental violations. The project has left a huge stain on the Workers' Party, two of whose leaders – Luiz Inácio Lula da Silva ('Lula') and Dilma Rousseff – made it a top priority of their administrations.

Oblivious to political events in Brazil, Chagas and Dias are now poor. Chagas, who had never thought of retiring because he 'didn't need to', has gone on a state pension so he can feed his wife, youngest daughter and grandson. After paying rent and electricity, which consume 70 per cent of his income, they are left with R$1.60 a day per person (about $0.45).

Located on the Xingu River, Altamira is a typical Amazonian city: almost all its trees have been cut because the local political and

ELIANE BRUM is a Brazilian journalist, writer and documentarist. She has worked for many years for the newspaper *Zero Hora* and the magazine *Época*. Since 2013 she has written a column in the Spanish paper *El País*. Her documentary film *Uma História Severina* (2005), co-directed with Debora Diniz, won numerous awards, while *Laerte-se* (2017), co-directed with Lygia Barbosa, about the transgender comic book artist Laerte Coutinho, was the first Brazilian production for Netflix. Her collection of essays *The Collector of Leftover Souls* was published in English in 2019 (Graywolf Press, USA/Granta, UK).

> 'When the new dam's reservoir began filling up and the water began to rise around their island, Chagas witnessed forest creatures dying. Monkeys, agoutis, armadillos and sloths dived from the forest into the water.'

economic elite view them as roadblocks or something to 'clean up'. The heat index (which takes account of temperature and humidity) tops 40 degrees Centigrade in summer and climbs above 30 degrees even during the winter rainy season. The couple have neither a refrigerator nor a fan. The centrepiece of their living room is a photomontage of their youngest daughter and two grandsons, a princess and two soldiers against a fake Disney backdrop.

When the new dam's reservoir began filling up and the water began to rise around their island, Chagas witnessed forest creatures dying. Monkeys, agoutis, armadillos and sloths dived from the forest into the water. 'We managed to save a few by pulling them into the canoe, but we saw a lot die,' he says. They are part of the forest, like him; like them, he has yet to find terra firma and feels as if he's drowning in the loneliness of the city. The hardships of his urban life aside, he took in two puppies because he says he doesn't know how to 'live without animals'. He borrowed money for powdered milk to feed them.

Now theirs is a life of firsts: the first electricity bill, the first rented home, the first time they needed to buy what they eat, the first hunger. Chagas wakes before 4 a.m. feeling suffocated and rushes to the backyard, a cement slab that has no trees but where he can glimpse a piece of sky. He doesn't sit because he doesn't have a chair. He stands, clinging to this shard of freedom, sometimes crying. 'Being poor is living in hell,' he says.

'I WAS KING'

Raimundo Braga Gomes is harsher: 'On the river, I was king.'

He and Chagas are *ribeirinhos*, traditional people of the forest, and one of the most invisible, misunderstood populations in Brazil. *Ribeirinhos* have a singular identity, defined by their intimate relationship with forest and river. They do not own the land, they belong to it. This is 'walking on wealth', as Gomes puts it. 'I didn't need money to live happy. My whole house was nature. The timber, straw, didn't need any nails. I had my patch of land where I planted a bit of everything, all sorts of fruit trees. I'd catch my fish, make manioc flour. If I wanted something else to eat, I'd grab a hen I'd raised. If I wanted meat, I'd hunt in the forest. And, to make money, I'd fish some more and sell it in town. I raised my three daughters, proud of what I was. I was rich.'

Like Gomes, most *ribeirinhos* descend either from poor Northeasterners taken to the forest to harvest latex in the late 19th century or from Second World War-era 'rubber soldiers' (a wartime Brazilian government programme in which workers were taken to the Amazon region to harvest rubber that was then supplied to the USA). When the rubber market crashed and the war ended, the bosses abandoned them in the woods. Some made families with indigenous women, occasionally stealing them from their villages. They began leading lives as fluid as the river: first on one bank, then another, shaping a unique experience. Even *ribeirinhos* of indigenous origin are different. They are not farmers, but they till the land. They fish, crack Brazil nuts, hunt, tap rubber and, on occasion, try their hand at prospecting. They live between worlds.

Accustomed to changing islands and indifferent to the concept of land as merchandise, they often confound people when they proclaim their freedom. 'I've never had a job,' says Chagas. 'Always been free.' They all work hard because forest life is tough, but they only do what they want, when they want. Converting them into the urban poor drains them of their essence.

It also makes them pariahs because they cannot find employment. Once proud of their freedom, they find themselves forced to live off odd jobs and favours. Significantly, they call the city 'outside'. 'I know everything on the river. Outside I know nothing,' says Chagas. 'Who's going to give me a job?'

Until recently *ribeirinhos* were not recognised as a traditional people by the government or by Norte Energia, the public–private consortium overseeing the dam. One day in 2012 Gomes was startled to see strangers arrive in a motorboat, men 'from the company'. They said his island was going to be 'removed'. He replied, 'I won't leave.' Then they told him his island would be underwater soon – it was sign or go down with it. 'I signed a document. But I can't read. I only know how to draw my name.'

Gomes was moved into one of the near-identical homes that Norte Energia constructed to house Belo Monte's expelled families. His neighbourhood was named Blue Water – ironic, given that it lies more than six kilometres from the river. That's much further away than the 1.5 or so kilometres stipulated in the construction agreement, which also says the

THE TRANS-AMAZONIAN HIGHWAY

In the early 1970s, when the propaganda put out by the military regime led by Emílio Garrastazu Médici was at its height, there was much talk of the *milagre brasileiro*, the Brazilian miracle, focused on the creation of state-owned enterprises and major infrastructure projects. The government's rallying cry was national integration, and to integrate, Brazil needed roads. But when the BR-230 – known as the Rodovia Transamazônica, the Trans-Amazonian Highway – was begun in 1972 it represented more than just a road; it was a long-standing dream of conquest, a challenge to the main resource the regime had at its disposal: the forest. Designed to cut across the widest part of the nation from east to west, it was intended to run for over eight thousand kilometres to the Peruvian border. It stopped after a little more than five thousand, parts of which are still unsurfaced. To this day, from October to March, particularly in the state of Pará, these stretches are subject to flooding and become impassable. That they have remained unmetalled is perhaps a blessing, because the frontier opened up by the Rodovia paved the way for the chainsaws, which is why environmentalists have fought to prevent the work from being completed, even though the road has helped to connect cities and areas that were previously unreachable. The Transamazônica was designed to be a concrete expression of the protectionist, nationalist slogan *integrar para não entregar*, integrate so we don't lose it (to foreign interests), along with a plan to populate these areas and exploit the natural resources. The slogan and the idea have been dusted off by Jair Bolsonaro's government, which has gone back to thinking of the 'green desert' as a frontier to conquer and a propaganda opportunity.

NUMBER OF MURDERS

Brazil has the highest number of homicides in the world, followed by India; the peak was in 2017 and numbers have been decreasing since.

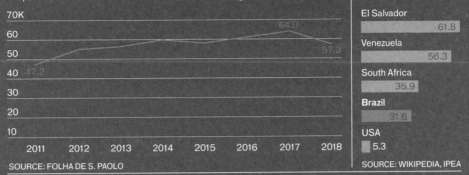

SOURCE: FOLHA DE S. PAOLO

HOMICIDE RATES

Per 100,000 inhabitants (2017)

El Salvador
61.8

Venezuela
56.3

South Africa
35.9

Brazil
31.6

USA
5.3

SOURCE: WIKIPEDIA, IPEA

NUMBER OF MURDERS BY ETHNICITY AND GENDER

Per 100,000 inhabitants

- Women not of colour
- Men not of colour
- Women of colour
- Men of colour

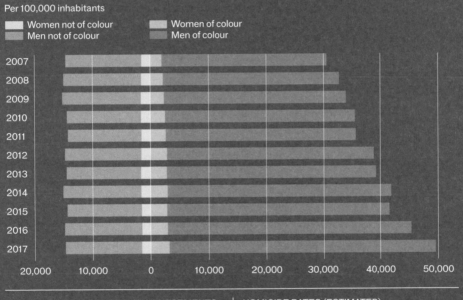

VIOLENCE IS INCREASING WITH INVESTMENTS IN LARGE PROJECTS IN AMAZONIA

Marabá
Altamira
Rio de Janeiro
São Paolo

SOURCE: IPEA, WIKIPEDIA, AMAZÔNIA SUSTENTÁVEL, METRÓPOLES

HOMICIDE RATES (ESTIMATED)

Per 100,000 inhabitants

Altamira   Brazil

Year	Altamira	Brazil
2012	77.6	29.4
2013	90.9	28.6
2014	98.5	29.8
2015	106.5	28.9
2016	91.1	30.6
2017	133.7	31.6

'On the River, I Was King'

'Returning home one Sunday Ribeiro waited in vain for her husband then eventually went out to search for him. When she found him he was naked, his head smashed by bricks and his tongue pulled out.'

houses must be varied and built with quality materials. After the walls started cracking, the courts suspended work on the dam until the dwellings could be brought into compliance. In the meantime Gomes watches as the cracks burrow deeper into his walls and roof.

'Now I'm poor. I have to buy everything I need,' he says. 'Since I don't have money to buy what I want, I buy what I can. I like manioc flour, but I can only afford rice. I used to harvest four hundred good watermelons, but today I can't buy even a bad one. I used to pick the hen I wanted to eat, but today I can't buy one. I used to have a living river, today I have a dead lake – and to get there I have to pay for transportation.'

'I LIVE AMONG DRUG DEALERS NOW'
Gomes decided to defy the monotony of lookalike houses by adding wooden lean-tos in the *ribeirinho* way. While he was working, a passer-by shouted, 'Hey, it's already got that poverty look!'

'You'll never understand my style,' Gomes shot back. Later, he added, 'Know what being poor is? It's having no choice.'

He has also learned that being poor means 'bullets are always shattering your windows'. Since 2000 Altamira's population has climbed from 77,000 to 111,000, a rise of about 44 per cent. Over the same period the murder rate skyrocketed 1,110 per cent.

The 2019 Atlas of Violence – published by the Institute for Applied Economic Research, a Brazilian public think tank – ranked Altamira as Brazil's second-most violent large city with an annual murder rate of 133.7 deaths per 100,000 people. By contrast, the rate is 35.6 in Rio de Janeiro. Both the rising population and the murder boom are in part attributable to Belo Monte, which drew thousands to a city without adequate infrastructure and has profoundly disrupted its social structure.

For *ribeirinhos*, who used to live a life without doors, the effect has been devastating. 'I'm living among drug dealers now. Once in a while there's a body on the ground. I counted thirteen that I saw myself. There're others I don't see. One Sunday alone it was two of the neighbour's boys. I just heard the pop, pop, pop,' says Gomes, imitating the sound of bullets. 'They tossed us into a field of violence.'

At least forty thousand people were torn from their homes so Belo Monte could be built. Roughly 1,500 are *ribeirinhos*. There are also farmers, fishermen and urban residents who lived in areas flooded by the dam. Some received cash payments, others relocation credit; still others were resettled. There were also those who got nothing and are fighting in the courts for reparations. The subdivisions that were built to house the displaced families have splintered neighbourhood bonds and jumbled together people who had never before lived side by side. They also mixed in members of rival drug factions that formerly kept to their own turf and overnight found themselves next-door neighbours.

In less than four years these 'collective

urban resettlements' have been transformed into Altamira's new territory of violence. Not only are the residents routinely subjected to robberies, hold-ups and murders but they must also bear the stigma of being labelled 'criminals'.

Eliza Ribeiro, forty-seven, lived with her husband on a small island. When they were cast into the city he couldn't find a job. 'My husband got desperate because we were going hungry, and he started drinking heavily,' she says. He also got involved with drug traffickers.

During the 2016 elections, Ribeiro, a fisherwoman, thought she couldn't get any poorer. She handed out flyers for one of Altamira's mayoral candidates and waved political banners on street corners for R$50 a day (c. $13.50 in 2019). Returning home one Sunday she waited in vain for her husband then eventually went out to search for him. When she found him he was naked, his head smashed by bricks and his tongue pulled out.

She saw her life contract. 'When I go to bed I never know what we're going to eat the next day. My youngest daughter wakes up crying and asks for food. I tell her, "Your dad died. I don't have any money." And I cry, too,' she says. One day she went knocking door to door. They offered her R$20 ($5.50) and a plate of food to clean the house and wash clothes. 'And my kids, what are they going to eat?' she asked, and went home to be hungry with her children.

She returned to fishing, but the six-kilometre journey to the river costs dearly in transportation and petrol. She and her daughter load everything they can – from gas canister to mattress – on a motorcycle and tuck her daughter's toddler in front. Clinging to the bike, and then a boat, the family takes four hours to reach a friend's island. There they put up a tarpaulin and hang hammocks.

SPILLING THE BEANS:
COFFEE AND OTHER RESOURCES

Sailing along the Brazilian coastline, early expeditions caught sight of the Atlantic Forest, which became the source of great wealth in the form of a tree with red wood that looked as if it had been cooked over hot coals (*brasa* in Portuguese, which perhaps accounts for the name pau-brasil, or brazilwood in English). In Europe it was used to dye cloth, and, thanks to the tree, the verdant land over the ocean became known as Brazil. Great wealth and then great poverty came from the *seringueira*, or rubber tree. In late 1896 the Amazonas Theatre was inaugurated in Manaus, a Renaissance-style temple of opera in the middle of the forest. It was tangible proof of the city's opulence during the peak of the rubber boom, one that would last only until the outbreak of the First World War. Then another tree became the driver of a cycle of wealth: the cacao tree, which became the principal resource of Bahia state for almost a century, for a time making Brazil the world's largest producer of the beans that are the basic ingredient of chocolate. Production in Bahia crashed in the late 1980s following an outbreak of a fungal infection, devastating the region's economy. During that same period Brazilians grew rich on coffee, production of which fuelled the growth of the city of São Paolo, in part because of the numbers of immigrants who arrived to work on the harvest of the precious berries. The current resource is oil, particularly following the discovery in 2008–9 of the pre-salt underwater oilfields off the coast of Rio state.

Above: The unregulated growth of the city of São Paulo contributes to the pollution of its rivers.
Below: The Traição hydroelectric plant – built on the Pinheiros River close to the Engenheiro Ari Torres Bridge – was inaugurated in 1940.

> 'Critics see the conversion of the forest peoples into the urban poor as no accidental tragedy but rather a political strategy.'

Five exhausting days of fishing later she returns to town for a few days to sell her fish and then repeats the operation.

Hordes of these motorbikes, often laden with entire families and usually helmetless, can be seen in Altamira, weaving around the air-conditioned double-cab pickup trucks with their lone drivers – a sight that epitomises the social tension in the cities of the Amazon.

RESISTANCE

Critics see the conversion of the forest peoples into the urban poor as no accidental tragedy but rather a political strategy. As a traditional people the *ribeirinhos* have a constitutionally guaranteed right to their way of life. When they are transformed into residents of the periphery they lose this right. On the one hand, the forests they once occupied are freed for construction, mining, agriculture and raising livestock; on the other, they become part of the enfeebled urban masses who will support any major incursion into the forest if it holds the possibility of a job.

Since democracy was reclaimed in Brazil, the pressure has never been greater to relax environmental laws and open forests up to exploitation. It's a tough moment. But it is also the first time that *ribeirinhos* expelled by a mega-project have forged a resistance movement of real size. Recently a group of them went to Brasília to lodge an unprecedented demand: the creation of a '*ribeirinho* territory' for around three hundred families along the Xingu River. They refuse to continue as urban poor. They demand, in effect, a kind of 'un-conversion' back to their lives as forest people.

As a result of their fight, the company has already been forced to provide some of them a monthly stipend to guarantee minimum support until the matter is settled. 'Norte Energia complies with all determinations laid out in the Basic Environmental Project,' the company said in a statement to the *Guardian* newspaper (UK), 'which calls for measures to monitor and mitigate long-term social and environmental impacts in areas of direct or indirect influence of the Belo Monte hydroelectric power plant. The document is validated by public and federal agencies.'

Leonardo Batista, fifty-eight, is one of the *ribeirinho* leaders and a member of the Ribeirinho Council. Better known as Aranô, he is son of a *ribeirinho* and an indigenous woman from the Juruna tribe. He lives in Jatobá, another urban resettlement, where he survives on R$50 a month. He only had something to eat on Christmas Day because his pastor sent him a plate of food. His house has been broken into three times. In December Aranô grew so desperate that he picked up his *borduna*, an indigenous weapon, and entered a meeting ready to capture the world's attention by busting things up. He was barred.

His tears make a river down his cheeks when he says, 'We've always had the before, the now, the after. The before has gone, the now is a nightmare. And the after?' ✒

Tales from Another Brazil

VALERIO MILLEFOGLIE
Translated by Alan Thawley

Typing 'Brazilian bar' into a search engine returns several hundred million hits in less than a second. You discover that Brazil is everywhere, and the windows of these bars look out on to every corner of the world. There has, for example, been a little slice of Brazil in the German city of Bonn since 1997, as we learn from the welcome sign at the Limão Brasil Bar & Restaurant. 'Autumn and the dark nights have returned, but don't worry, the Favela is always an oasis of warmth in the cold,' say the team at Bar Favela in Helsinki. The letters of the word *favela* feature on six of the columns that form the façade of the bar, and when they are lit up at night they help to draw people in. Inside is a world of yellow, green and red, and you'll find live music here sometimes. 'We are in Las Vegas, but we're in a mall; you can see shoppers walking past the windows,' says Brandon Santo of the Pampas Brazilian Grille. A stone's throw from the Las Vegas amusement arcade in Sofia is Botequim da Sil, which describes itself as the best Brazilian bar in the whole of Bulgaria. Vienna, meanwhile, has its Carioca Bar. 'We have huge windows,' says owner Livia Mata, 'so I watch people passing by on foot, on bikes, in their cars, and I also have a view of the Danube Canal.' There's an imaginary river inside the Carioca Bar: on a white wall, next to one of the windows, hang eight colourful wooden boats sailing upstream towards the ceiling. The Rio Grande Bar is in Bellinzona, the capital of the Swiss canton of Ticino. According to Nanad Bozovich, the Serbian waiter who

me Chico Buarque songs,' she recalls. 'There had been plans to demolish this area of town. We're in the old centre, and at the time, twenty-eight years ago, there were only three bars. One of them was the Samboa. I decided to buy this building because to my eyes the street, Via delle Caserme, was like a corner of Pelourinho, the historic district of Salvador in Bahia. The slave trade began in Pelourinho, and today it's one of the main centres of capoeira. There they had the gibbet where they used to hang the slaves, whereas this was once the site of the Bagno Borbonico, the old prison. The bar is between the Museum of the People of Abruzzo and the houses where the poet Gabriele D'Annunzio and the writer Ennio Flaiano were born. We're not by the sea, there's no sea view, but we have the River Pescara that divides the modern city from the old town. In any case, when we're in the bar we can hear the sound of the ocean. I remember one year when there was a heavy snowfall, people ordered caipirinhas and then went outside with their glasses into the snowy street. Everything, every ornament, every picture, every tile comes from Brazil.' And over the years there have been visitors from Brazil, too: Caetano Veloso, Gilberto Gil, Toquinho, Irio de Paula; right after playing at the Pescara International Jazz Festival they came for jam sessions at the Samboa. A photograph from 1998 shows Stefania with Veloso. 'I was feeling emotional in that photo because I'd just told him and his promoter Gilda that I'd fallen in love with Brazil reading the poetry of Vinicius de Moraes. At that point, Gilda took a photo out of her bag and told me, "I spent my life with this man."' The man was Moraes, who died in 1980. 'I live in a tropical country,' Stefania concludes, quoting Sérgio Mendes's song 'País Tropical'. And that country is, of course, her bar.

has lived in the city for forty years, 'On one side the restaurant is flanked by a number of banks, but on the other is a ten-storey apartment building; in the evenings we see the residents going about their private lives, and they see our car park.' He goes on to explain how the Rio Grande came to be set up in Switzerland. 'The owner took a holiday in Brazil years ago and came back so much in love with the place that he wanted to bring his happy memories home with him.' Next stop, South Wimbledon in London, and the Little Brazil Bar & Restaurant, where you can eat with a view of Rio's statue of Christ the Redeemer – as wallpaper. And with a little imagination you can even create a new homeland for yourself, as Stefania Di Blasio has done at the Samboa Salsa Bar in the Italian city of Pescara. 'When I was a girl I told people I'd been born in Brazil. My mother passed away saying, "Stop telling people you were born in Brazil." My babysitter used to sing

An Author Recommends

A book, a film and an album
to understand Brazil,
chosen by:

LUIZ RUFFATO
Translated by Laura Garmeson

The son of immigrants from Portugal and Italy,
Luiz Ruffato is a journalist and author. In his work
he describes a Brazil far from the familiar stereotypes, and his most recent title to be translated
into English, *There Were Many Horses* (Amazon
Crossing, 2014), is an experimental novel that
describes one day in the life of the city of São
Paolo from multiple perspectives. He is one of
the founders of the Igreja do Livro Transformador
('Church of the Transforming Book'), a secular
movement that encourages reading in Brazil. In
2013 his novel *Domingos Sem Deus* ('Sundays
Without God') earned him the prestigious Casa
de las Américas award.

THE BOOK
NOWHERE PEOPLE
Paulo Scott
And Other Stories
2014

Curiously, Brazilian literature, in contrast to that of Hispanic America, has never been a prolific producer of political novels. Even the long period in the shadow of the dictatorship (1964–85) is rarely explored by Brazilian fiction writers. For this reason the publication of *Nowhere People* (Portuguese title *Habitante Irreal*) by Paulo Scott (b. 1966) in 2011 was very welcome. It is a novel that bravely confronts the moral dilemmas of the Brazilian left, which came to power with the election of Luiz Inácio Lula da Silva in 2002, and foregrounds the issues affecting Brazil's indigenous population, who otherwise tend to be completely absent from the nation's fiction. Narrated in the third person, the novel begins in 1989 – the year of the first presidential elections after the military regime – when we are introduced to Paulo, a 21-year-old activist with the left-wing PT (the Brazilian Workers' Party) who has grown disillusioned with party politics.

He falls in love with Maína, a fourteen-year-old indigenous girl, who becomes pregnant with his child. After trying to help her family, who live in poverty by the side of a road, he renounces everything and flees to London. Enter Donato – their mixed-heritage son, abandoned by Paulo and orphaned after his mother's death then adopted by a couple of professors – who is now trying to find meaning in his life. Through the plot Scott reflects on and interrogates the ethical and moral problems inherent in the collective decisions that form part of our recent history in Brazil and which could be seen to have foreshadowed the horrors we are witnessing now with the rise of the far right embodied in the figure of Jair Bolsonaro and his politics of hatred and intolerance. The book, winner of the Machado de Assis Prize, has been translated into English, German and Croatian.

Quantity can often generate quality. Since 1995 Brazilian cinema has seen a substantial increase in the numbers of movies produced: 185 films were released in Brazil in 2018, some of which attracted international attention. Strangely, very few of them explore the lives of the lower middle classes – they tend either to be romantic comedies, farces or films about confrontations between police and drug traffickers set in the *favelas*. One of the few films to depict the world of work is *Arábia* (2017), written and directed by Affonso Uchôa and João Dumans with cinematography by Leonardo Feliciano. The story follows Cristiano (played by the wonderful Aristides de Sousa), who has just left prison and is trying to get his life back on track as he searches for work across the state of Minas Gerais. Eventually he settles in the city of Ouro Preto – not among its tourist attractions, which include one of the best-preserved baroque monuments in the world, but in the industrial zones on the outskirts, a landscape of bleak metalworks, melancholy small towns and inhabitants who have lost all hope. Punctuated by a voiceover, the film's narration underscores the poetic atmosphere of this mythical journey in search of a redemption that remains forever out of reach, because Cristiano, like the other characters he encounters on the road, has always been condemned to a life of solitude, failure and anonymity, purely as a result of living in a country where inequality creates unfathomable gulfs. Uchôa and Dumans reached a rare level of aesthetic perfection while at the same time producing a scathing social critique that demonstrates a deep respect for and uncommon understanding of a side of Brazil usually ignored by the world of cinema.

Although Brazil continues to exist in the international imagination predominantly as the country of bossa nova, a movement rooted in the 1950s and 1960s, many people also associate it with MPB (música popular brasileira), the golden years of which were the 1970s and 1980s. Unlike bossa nova, which portrayed Brazil through the optimistic lens of post-war democracy, MPB took the aesthetic refinement of bossa nova (which was essentially a sophisticated reinterpretation of samba) and infused it with a message to combat the twenty-plus-year military dictatorship. People who want to understand the country in terms of its socio-political issues today should turn to the rap scene that developed on the peripheries of the big cities, since most Brazilian music these days is dominated by the mainstream cultural industry and hamstrung by its pursuit of commercial success. I suggest they start with Racionais MC's, who emerged in the late 1980s and managed to reach audiences outside their communities while never losing sight of their roots as they vehemently denounced society's injustices. Their songs, which are true narratives in verse, describe life for the impoverished youth marginalised by racism and class prejudice, seen from the inside looking out. Themes such as organised crime, police violence, drug use and social exclusion feature throughout their discography from which I would recommend their double album, *1000 Trutas 1000 Tretas* (*truta* and *treta* being slang terms for friend and confusion). The album is a recording of one of their live shows from 2006 and features fifteen of the best tracks from their two previous albums, *Sobrevivendo no Inferno* (1997) and *Nada Como um Dia Após o Outro Dia* (2002).

The Playlist

ALBERTO RIVA
Translated by Alan Thawley

Listen to this playlist at:
open.spotify.com/user/iperborea

W hen it comes to music, Brazil is not just one country but many – Brazilian music takes many forms, and diversity is its brand. If there is a single source, a mother lode, it is samba – the music born of the slave trade, the rhythm that began as African and became Brazilian. But samba was already the result of refinement and intellectualisation, even when it came from the *favela* and was played by a fishmonger. In the 1950s and 1960s samba became ever more refined, and bossa nova was born. A style and a revolution that led to the emergence of singer-songwriters and Brazilian rock over the next three decades.

In the 2000s that first development and its successors became highly fragmented, still honouring the legacy of the past but also focused on the present. In twelve steps: Chico Buarque, who returned to political songwriting in 2018; Caetano and his three sons, coming out of the past to move onwards into the future; Céu's electronic pop; Vanessa da Mata's sophisticated pop; the samba-tinged pop of Roberta Sá; the samba-pop of Rogé; Nina Wirtti's respect for tradition with her samba-choro; the samba-philosophy of Marcos Sacramento. All of them have beautiful voices. Using her voice to express a poetic vision, Adriana Calcanhotto is a direct heir to Caetano, just as Thiago Amud channels the combined legacy of Caetano and Chico when he adds portraits and satire. These artists continue the tradition of the Brazilian song with the same taste for words as the rappers Criolo and Emicida, who might at first appear worlds away from the others were it not for a collective spirit that brings them together: samba once again. Because samba is not just a rhythm, for Brazilian musicians it is a way of life. Whether *favelado* or bourgeois, the *sambista* is always at odds with society.

1
Emicida
Casa
2015

2
Thiago Amud
*Plano de
Carreira*
2018

3
Céu
*Sobre o Amor
e Seu Trabalho
Silencioso*
2009

4
Rogê
*Suingue
do Samba*
2016

5
Criolo
*Não Existe
Amor em SP*
2011

6
Caetano
Veloso (et al.)
O Seu Amor
2018

7
Chico
Buarque
As Caravanas
2017

8
Marcos
Sacramento
Pavio
2009

9
Nina Wirtti
Zé Ponte
2014

10
Vanessa
da Mata
Ilegais
2007

11
Roberta Sá
Feito Carnaval
2015

12
Adriana
Calcanhotto
Programa
2002

Further Reading

FICTION

Caio Fernando Abreu
Whatever Happened to Dulce Veiga?
University of Texas Press, 2000

Jorge Amado
Captains of the Sands
Penguin, 2013

Jorge Amado
Dona Flor and Her Two Husbands
Vintage, 2006

Martha Batalha
The Invisible Life of Euridice Gusmao
Oneworld, 2017

Chico Buarque
Spilt Milk
Atlantic Books, 2013 (UK)
Grove Press, 2013 (USA)

Rubem Fonseca
Winning the Game and Other Stories
Tagus Press, 2013

Daniel Galera
Blood-Drenched Beard
Penguin, 2015

Milton Hatoum
The Brothers
Farrar, Straus and Giroux, 2002

Paulo Lins
City of God
Bloomsbury, 2006 (UK)
Black Cat, 2006 (USA)

Clarice Lispector
Near to the Wild Heart
Penguin, 2014 (UK)
New Directions, 2012 (USA)

Machado de Assis
Dom Casmurro
Peter Owen, 2016

Ana Paula Maia
Saga of Brutes
Dalkey Archive, 2016

Geovani Martins
The Sun on My Head: Stories
Faber & Faber, 2019 (UK)
Farrar, Straus and Giroux, 2019 (USA)

Raduan Nassar
A Cup of Rage
Penguin, 2016 (UK)
New Directions, 2017 (USA)

Alexandre Vidal Porto
Sergio Y.
Europa Editions, 2016

Luiz Ruffato
There Were Many Horses
Amazon Crossing, 2014

Rodrigo de Souza Leão
All Dogs Are Blue
And Other Stories, 2013

Cristovão Tezza
The Eternal Son
Scribe, 2013

Mario Vargas Llosa
The War of the End of the World
Faber & Faber, 2012 (UK)
Picador, 2008 (USA)

NON-FICTION

Alex Bellos
Futebol: The Brazilian Way of Life
Bloomsbury, 2014

Eliane Brum
*The Collector of Leftover Souls: Dispatches
from Brazil* (UK) / *The Collector of
Leftover Souls: Field Notes on Brazil's
Everyday Insurrections* (USA)
Granta, 2019 (UK)
Graywolf Press, 2019 (USA)

Sérgio Buarque de Holanda
Roots of Brazil
University of Notre Dame Press, 2012

Alex Cuadros
*Brazillionaires: The Godfathers of
Modern Brazil* (UK) / *Brazillionaires:
Wealth, Power, Decadence, and Hope
in an American Country* (USA)
Profile Books, 2016 (UK)
Spiegel & Grau, 2016 (USA)

Misha Glenny
*Nemesis: The Hunt for Brazil's Most
Wanted Criminal* (UK) / *Nemesis: One Man
and the Battle for Rio's Biggest Slum* (USA)
Vintage, 2016 (UK)
Vintage, 2017 (USA)

David Grann
*The Lost City of Z: A Tale of Deadly
Obsession in the Amazon*
Simon & Schuster, 2017 (UK)
Knopf Doubleday, 2010 (USA)

Rudyard Kipling
Brazilian Sketches
Abandoned Bookshop (Kindle edition), 2016

Davi Kopenawa and Bruce Albert
*The Falling Sky: Words
of a Yanomami Shaman*
Harvard University Press, 2013

Luiz Eduardo Soares
Rio de Janeiro: Extreme City
Penguin, 2016

Caetano Veloso
*Tropical Truth: A Story of Music
and Revolution in Brazil*
Bloomsbury, 2003 (UK)
Da Capo Press, 2003 (USA)

Stefan Zweig
Brazil: A Land of the Future
Ariadne Press, 2000

Graphic design and art direction: Tomo Tomo and Pietro Buffa

Photography: André Liohn
The photographic content was curated by Prospekt Photographers.

Illustrations: Edoardo Massa

Infographics and cartography: Pietro Buffa

Managing editor (English-language edition): Simon Smith

Thanks to: Martina Barlassina, Otávio Costa, Adriana Costanzo, Fabio Muzi Falconi, Marcelo Ferroni, Roberto Francavilla, Ana Paula Hisayama, Cassiano Elek Machado, Marcelo Marzola, Rita Mattar, MC Carol, Flávio Moura, Stephanie Nolen, Thais Pahl, Paulo Roberto Pires, Eliane Ramos, Lorenzo Ribaldi, Fernando Rinaldi, Alberto Riva, Bianca Rizzi, Luana Rizzi, Elisa Rossi

The opinions expressed in this publication are those of the authors and do not purport to reflect the views and opinions of the publishers.

http://europaeditions.com/thepassenger
http://europaeditions.co.uk/thepassenger
#ThePassengerMag

The Passenger – Brazil
© Iperborea S.r.l., Milan, and Europa Editions, 2020

Translators: Laura Garmeson (Portuguese), Stephen Smithson (German), Alan Thawley (Italian), Diane Grosklaus Whitty (Portuguese 'On the River, I Was King')
All translations © Iperborea S.r.l., Milan, and Europa Editions, 2020 except 'On the River, I Was King' © Guardian News & Media Ltd, 2019

ISBN: 9781787702417

All Rights Reserved. No part of this publication may be reproduced, stored in a retrieval system or transmitted in any form or by any means without the written permission of the publishers and copyright owners.

The moral rights of the authors and other copyright-holders are hereby asserted in accordance with the Copyright Designs and Patents Act 1988.

Printed on Munken Pure thanks to the support of Arctic Paper

Printed by ELCOGRAF S.p.A., Verona, Italy

A Sign of the Times: The Copan
© Fabian Federl, 2019. First published in Die Zeit under the title 'Wieder gut in Form' on 17 January 2019.

Order and Progress?
© Jon Lee Anderson, 2019. First published in The New Yorker under the title 'Jair Bolsonaro's Southern Strategy' on 25 March 2019, used by permission of the Wylie Agency (UK) Ltd.

Funk, Pride and Prejudice
© Alberto Riva, 2019

Prime Time
© Alex Cuadros, 2016. All rights reserved. First published in the USA by Spiegel & Grau, an imprint of Random House, part of Penguin Random House LLC, New York, and by Profile Books (UK) in the book Brazillionaires.

Prosperity Now
© Anna Virginia Balloussier, 2019

In Defence of Fragmentation
© Michel Laub, 2019

The Road
© Stephanie Nolen, 2018. First published in The Globe and Mail on 26 January 2018.

Real Life on the Passarela do Samba
© Aydano André Motta, 2019

The War is a chapter from the book A Guerra by Bruno Paes Manso and Camila Nunes Dias, published in 2018 by Todavia Editora, São Paolo. © Bruno Paes Manso, Camila Nunes Dias, 2018.

You've Got Mail!
© Fabian Federl, 2019. First published in Annabelle under the title 'Die Post Ist Da!' in June 2019.

'On the River, I Was King'
© Guardian News & Media Ltd, 2019. First published in the Guardian under the title 'They Owned an Island, Now They Are the Urban Poor: The Tragedy of Altamira' on 6 February 2018.